Redesigning Education
Shaping Learning Systems Around the Globe

Innovation Unit
for The Global Education Leaders' Program

booktrope

2013
Seattle, Washington

Copyright 2013 Innovation Unit

www.gelponline.org

First published 2013

ISBN: 978-1-62015-132-7
epub ISBN: 978-1-62015-121-1

For further information regarding permissions, please contact
info@booktrope.com

Library of Congress Control Number: 2013937270

The views in this book reflect those of the authors and not necessarily of the Bill & Melinda Gates Foundation

ACKNOWLEDGMENTS

This book has been written by the team of Innovation Unit consultants and researchers who lead and learn from the Global Education Leaders' Program on behalf of its members and partners.

We are: David Albury, Al Bertani, Martha Hampson, Valerie Hannon, David Jackson, Anthony Mackay, Amelia Peterson and Julie Temperley. Libby Scarlett designed the book. Lynn Olson, the Advisor to the Director of College Ready, US Programs at the Bill & Melinda Gates Foundation, edited the volume.

We would like to thank our colleagues at the Innovation Unit who have contributed their time and perspective to challenge and support us, in particular Rajwinder Cheema, John Craig, Katharine Smith and Gareth Wynne.

Innovation Unit is a London-based social enterprise committed to using the power of innovation to solve social challenges. We support leaders and organizations who deliver public services to see and do things differently and to achieve radically different solutions that offer better outcomes for lower costs.

Four GELP members took time out of their busy working lives to read and review early drafts of this book. They are: Andrea Coleman, GELP NYC; Margery Evans, GELP Australia; Chris Kennedy, GELP British Columbia; and Kristiina Kumpulainen, GELP Finland. Many thanks for your critical friendship and guidance.

We'd like to extend our thanks to Riel Miller at UNESCO, whose recent evaluation of GELP made an invaluable contribution to our thinking.

We also would like to take this opportunity to thank our brilliant partners at the Bill & Melinda Gates Foundation, Cisco, Promethean and the Ellen Koshland Family Fund. GELP could not exist without your continuing expert and generous support and advocacy.

Finally, and most importantly, to the GELP jurisdictional teams and the individuals and organizations that comprise them, whose extraordinary leadership is the focus and foundation of this book. It is a privilege to work with you.

For more information about the Global Education Leaders Program visit www.gelponline.org

CONTENTS

INTRODUCTION

THE DEATH OF EDUCATION?

We are witnessing the death of education. The structures and strictures of school; learning from 9 til 3; learning on your own and not with other people— that's dead or dying. And learning is just beginning.[1]

Professor Stephen Heppell, October 2012

Open any number of publications by education thinkers and commentators, and you will encounter compelling arguments for radical change in the way countries, cities and states organize and provide learning. You will read brilliant critiques of the industrial model of schooling that has dominated education around the world for the last two centuries. And you will hear inspirational accounts of people and places demonstrating what learning in the 21st century could and should be.

Education, we are told, is becoming both learner centred and data driven; anytime and anywhere; personalised and collaborative; real world and practical; games based and simulated; formal and informal. While not mutually exclusive, some of these qualities are in tension; they can be contestable, competing and hard to get right.

We're also told that education can and must become more efficient and more productive. This is good news, given the number of jurisdictions disinvesting in public services, while others try to respond to exploding demand.

Education in the future also will be more diverse and inclusive. States will no longer have the monopoly in running school, interrupted here and there by fee-paying institutions available to a privileged few. Instead learning will be provided by business, philanthropists, social entrepreneurs, communities and faith groups, families and—most radical of all—learners themselves.

The three of us agree. A series of papers published between 2008 and 2010 argued for a learning society[2] in which a fundamental rethinking of what learning should look like,[3] new connections between different parts of the system[4] and the strategic and creative deployment of technology coalesce to offer a new vision for education: Education 3.0.[5]

The evidence is overwhelming. These changes are happening now, albeit unevenly and sporadically. As we hurtle through the second decade of the century, the pressure for mainstream education to change is becoming ever greater.

But there is a problem.

There is no version of this complex, exciting new world of learning that can arrive fully operational and ready to open for business on Monday morning. We need a disciplined process to move from an imperfect present to a preferred future. For good or ill, education systems exist—schools exist—and around the world every day schools open their doors to welcome inside millions of learners, mostly children. Hundreds of thousands of teachers and school leaders and administrators arrive at work. And whole communities of parents and families continue to support schools democratically—where the opportunity exists—and financially, through taxes or fees or both.

So while it's absolutely essential that thought leaders debate what learning should look like, how schools should operate and even what education is for in this century, we should at the same time and with the same degree of seriousness discuss how we get there; how we effect transformation from the education systems we have to the education systems we want and need. Furthermore, the leaders of existing education systems, who hold the responsibility and mandate for transformation, should shape that debate.

INTENTIONALITY AND COLLABORATION: THE GLOBAL EDUCATION LEADERS' PROGRAM

The Global Education Leaders' Program, or GELP, is a partnership of teams of education system leaders and world-class organizations collaborating in a global community to transform education in practice.

GELP's objectives are to:
• accelerate and sustain transformation within GELP members' 'local' systems and nations;
• develop transformational capacity and personal efficacy within education system leaders;
• advocate and continually refine a vision of 21st century teaching and learning; and
• facilitate an interactive and growing global community of education leaders and change agents.

GELP membership is diverse and dynamic. At the time of this writing, teams from twelve jurisdictions in nine countries on five continents participate. They are: Australia; Brazil; British Columbia, Canada; Chaoyang District, Beijing, China; Finland; India; New Zealand; South Korea; Victoria, Australia; and three jurisdictions from the United States: Colorado, Kentucky and New York City.

Among this group are jurisdictions that consistently achieve the highest rankings in international benchmarking. Others sometimes struggle to provide education for all in the face of extraordinary challenges. Members differ dramatically in scale, populations, budgets, governance, resources, curricula and testing regimes.

Every six months this extraordinary group gathers in one of their jurisdictions to share challenges and breakthroughs, to generate new ideas and plans and to reflect on and consolidate their learning. Between these global events, individual and cross jurisdictional work continues as teams explore a range of practical expressions of their transformational goals. Of course these vary from context to context, but they share in common:

• a focus on developing new pedagogy, curriculum and assessment;
• developing new roles for and relationships with learners and providers;
• planning key elements of system transformation, such as changing system conditions, developing leadership capacity and the workforce and engaging stakeholders.

Cisco's support for the Global Education Leaders Program reflects the company's long-standing belief that education is the foundation of stronger societies and more competitive economies. Fifteen years ago, Cisco created the Cisco Networking Academy, and since then, through the dramatic spread of the Academy into 165 countries around the world, we have provided networking and communications certifications to millions of young people. GELP has extended that idea, by showing how a broader set of student skills, such as problem-solving and collaboration, can be placed at the heart of school system transformation in developed and emerging countries alike. By understanding from the inside what innovative education looks like, and seeing how the most exciting new forms of learning are likely to develop, Cisco is able to create engaging, media-rich connected learning experiences for students that support and sustain visionary education in practice.

The Bill & Melinda Gates Foundation supports GELP because it believes every life has equal value and education is the pathway to opportunity. Through this global partnership, the Foundation can learn from and share best practices around the world and contribute to the exchange of ideas in a fluid, rapidly changing environment. Like the other partners in GELP, the Foundation believes that personalized learning for students and teachers, fuelled by technology, can dramatically accelerate learning in this century and make it more equitable and more accessible. The Foundation supports the participation of U.S. jurisdictions, like Colorado and Kentucky, in such innovation efforts.

Redesigning Education is a book about system transformation rooted in practice. It is about education systems and what it takes to transform them when the context within which they grew up and flourished fundamentally alters.

It is a book about system leaders who acknowledge that the arrangements for learning over which they preside on behalf of citizens no longer work for the vast majority of young people, and who seek to change that.

It is about what happens when such leaders join together in a global learning community—diverse, conflicted, uncertain—but determined to harness these and other qualities to learn from one another to transform their systems to meet the new challenges.

GELP began in 2009. In its first three years, the system leaders in GELP worked together, first and foremost, to *become* a community of learning and of practice—no small achievement in such a diverse and distributed group. As a community they have developed, refined and shared in their contexts a compelling and, critically, an *actionable* vision for the future of education: Education 3.0. They have devised strategies for moving toward that future and have developed roadmaps to describe and plan their route to system transformation.

Recently GELP has shifted gears. The jurisdictional teams and the system leaders who comprise them are now dealing with practical challenges as they move from ideation to implementation and transform their education systems for real.

In *Redesigning Education*, we set out some of the key ideas, models and practices that so far have informed and emerged from the work of the GELP community.

Redesigning Education concludes by drawing these lessons together in ways that could apply beyond the countries taking part in GELP. The conclusion also highlights some of the challenges that remain outstanding and will become increasingly important in the next stages of the GELP jurisdictions' journeys.

The three of us are proud to have travelled the journey so far with our colleagues in GELP and are excited about the opportunities and challenges we will face, together, in the next period.

Anthony Mackay, Vicki Phillips, Michael Stevenson
Co-chairs, the Global Education Leaders' Program

Anthony Mackay

Vicki Phillips

Michael Stevenson

GELP members gathered for the Global Event Helsinki, Finland 2012

Olli Häkämies

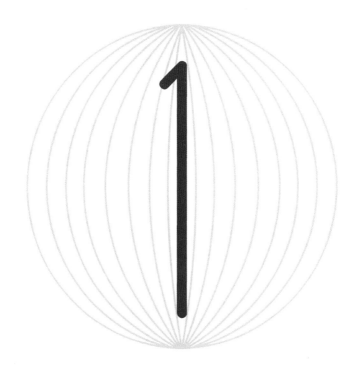

TRANSFORMING EDUCATION NOW: UNSTOPPABLE FORCES FOR CHANGE

The thrust for constant innovation has long prevailed in sectors such as technology and healthcare, but education has generally lacked this approach in both policymaking and the classroom. We face unprecedented global challenges— poverty, conflict, unemployment, inequality, environmental sustainability and others. Education is the route to short and long-term solutions, yet today's learning systems are not coping with the task.[6]

World Innovation Summit for Education

The new century has ushered in unimaginable change, from the Arab Spring to the global recession, from climate change to new uses and access to technology and media of all kinds. Yet here in the new century's second decade, the potential for education to help address changes in life, work and the nature of citizenship remains largely unrealized. As a result, a plethora of voices are demanding faster progress toward learning systems that equip all citizens with the knowledge, skills and dispositions to survive and thrive in the 21st century.

Influential writers, academics and researchers,[7,8] urge a radical and fundamental rethinking of the role of education:
...at a time when college degrees do not guarantee gainful employment or a meaningful life, what is the point of preparing someone to be ready for college? At a time when most of the careers for our children are yet to be invented, how could we prepare them? At a time when seven billion human beings live in

vastly different societies that are intricately connected, how could "all children be above average" or winners of the global competition in a narrowly defined game?[9]

Yong Zhao

Employers such as AT&T[10] in the United States and Telstra in Australia echo the need for transformation and assert a role for themselves in shaping and sometimes providing education. In a 2012 white paper on technology in education, Telstra noted:

As technologies continue to make their way from personal use into the broader work and learning environments, they offer great promise for creating significant improvements in generating, capturing and sharing knowledge; tapping into different sources of expertise; co-creating new learning experiences; and engaging key stakeholders more deeply in the educational process.[11]

Global organizations and non-profits have contributed to the ferment, including the OECD's Innovative Learning Environments project,[12] the World Bank,[13] the World Innovation Summit for Education (WISE),[14] the UN's Education First initiative,[15] UNESCO's Education for All program[16] and the Global Campaign for Education championed by former UK Prime Minister Gordon Brown.[17] All see education as part of the solution to peace and prosperity even in the poorest and most conflicted parts of the world.

Learning—not only schooling—is critical for children and youth to succeed. And learning for all—giving not just some but all children an opportunity to learn—is critical for a nation to prosper.[18]

World Bank

Students, communities, schools and teachers also have sounded the call, which is being answered by a raft of new learning providers. The next chapter, *Toward a Learning Ecosystem*, explores how the emergence of new entrants into education is ramping up the pressure on existing providers and accelerating transformation in unexpected ways.

Most notably, students, families, communities and entrepreneurs are creating their own learning models on the ground, while many governments continue, off pace,

to dictate change from above. Emerging forms of schooling and learning are not waiting for permission from government or authorities, as the rapid spread of new learning opportunities can attest.

Big Picture Learning[19] was formed as a non-profit organization in 1995 by two educators, Dennis Littky and Elliot Washor, who wanted to provide students with a personalized learning experience driven by their passions and anchored in internships out in the community two days a week. Today, there are Big Picture schools in the US, Canada, Australia, Israel and the Netherlands.

In 2006, financial analyst Salman Khan made a few YouTube videos to tutor his cousins in math and discovered that strangers began watching them and found them useful. Since then he has recorded 4,000 videos, which have been viewed over 240 million times, and "Khan Academy" has become a global phenomenon. The website is a charity, and all the content—which now extends beyond math to a whole range of other subjects—is free to access to any and all learners. Additionally, schools around the world are incorporating the videos and problem sets into mainstream classrooms.

Chapter 3, *Shifting Horizons*, explores more of the most exciting new learning opportunities to derive a set of design principles for learning that system leaders can use.

MAPPING AND NAVIGATING A NEW LANDSCAPE
The Global Education Leaders' Program (GELP) is in part a practical, problem solving solution to the urgency, scale and complexity of responding to these unstoppable forces for change that are altering and repopulating the landscape of education.

Leaders of education systems, confronted by these undeniable forces, must make a decision. They can try, Canute-like, to resist the tide and deny transformation.

Or, as the leaders of the education systems in GELP have done, they can try to shape the transformation of learning on behalf of their citizens to lead their systems consciously into the future and to share their transformational journeys together as a global learning community.

In taking on this responsibility, system leaders in GELP first needed to understand the nature of the challenge. This is complex and difficult, so to make a start they sought to explore the main drivers in their systems that are most relevant and urgent for education in their contexts. Simultaneously they set out to develop and refine a vision for what transformed education systems should be and do and the learning environments they should provide.

Much of the system leaders' early work in GELP focused on developing and refining these "cases for change" and their shared vision for the future of learning. The outcome is a compelling, practical expression of the challenge they face, comprising:

• a shared conceptualization of the **opportunities, challenges and pathways for young learners**; and
• a **unifying and galvanizing vision** for a transformed and deeply connected learning society: Education 3.0.

With this dual focus, system leaders in GELP are tackling what is *needed* and what is *possible*.

Image courtesy of India Study Hall

NEW OPPORTUNITIES, CHALLENGES AND PATHWAYS FOR YOUNG LEARNERS

... STUDENTS NEED TO BE CAPABLE NOT ONLY OF CONSTANTLY ADAPTING BUT ALSO OF CONSTANTLY LEARNING AND GROWING, OF POSITIONING THEMSELVES AND REPOSITIONING THEMSELVES IN A FAST CHANGING WORLD....[20]

OECD

The dominant shifts characterizing the 21st century provide both challenges and opportunities for learners. In developed economies, globalization, changing demographics and environmental unsustainability exert social and economic pressure but also open up opportunities for wider, richer routes through learning and employment. Educational underperformance and the need for a better return on investment have resulted in an explosion of invention—both from necessity and to meet demand. In contrast, many developing economies face a chronic need— and high demand—for low-cost, high-quality learning at scale and at speed. They seek innovative practices that can leapfrog costly stages of development. In both contexts, the need for social mobility, equity and economic improvement have ignited a new debate on local and global citizenship.

Digital technology provides enormous opportunities for powerful and effective collaboration. For learners the world over, opportunities abound in ways they have never before—fuelled not just by technology itself but by its ability to reimagine learning, teaching, schooling and of what it means to be a collaborative citizen. Changes to how people can learn are spawning adaptive new models. In responding to these challenges, communities, schools, students and "edupreneurs" are devising innovations that enrich learning and help continually redefine what education means.

The 10,000 students at Sweden's 36 Kunskapsskolan institutions are supported by teachers and parents to develop and pursue a personalized education plan. This begins with the setting of long-term attainment goals when they begin at the school, and is continued through weekly tutorial meetings to review and reflect on progress and to set new short-term aims and challenges. As in many schools, the KED education program developed by Kunskapsskolan uses an online virtual learning environment, which is accessible to students, teachers and parents. The difference is that students, not teachers, plan their day-to-day schedules and record their progress using an online log. Teachers upload students' results, tasks and comments in the school's online Pupil Documentation System, making it easy for parents to keep up with what their children are doing at school. When not in class, students are free to do much of their work at home, or can opt to study in one of each school's open-access "learning spaces." These spaces provide a range of facilities—from lecture halls to small study spaces—for students to use, giving them further autonomy in their approach to learning. Kunskapsskolan schools are consistently above average on Sweden's national assessments and outperform other Swedish schools serving similar demographics. The KED Education program is now being recreated in schools in India, the US and the UK, through partnerships between Kunskapsskolan and education entrepreneurs local to each country in for-profit business arrangements.

Image courtesy of Kunskapsskolan

The challenge for education systems is to adapt to these changes while providing learners with the capabilities to thrive in an increasingly networked world, where adaptability and the skill of learning itself are essential. These 21st century skills comprise:
• problem-solving and decision-making;
• creative and critical thinking;
• collaboration, communication and negotiation;
• intellectual curiosity and the ability to find, select, structure and evaluate information.

The Assessment & Teaching of 21st Century Skills project has captured these skills in four broad categories:[21]
Ways of thinking: creativity, critical thinking, problem-solving, decision-making and learning
Ways of working: communication and collaboration
Tools for working: information and communications technology and information literacy
Skills for living in the world: citizenship, life and career, and personal and social responsibility

The speed with which the world is changing beyond the classroom necessitates rethinking how, where and by whom learning takes place. Schooling must become an activity, not a place. And students must actively engage with the learning process itself to become life-long learners. Yet the dominant model of schooling remains largely that of 20th century knowledge transmission.

A UNIFYING AND GALVANIZING VISION
GELP has been animated by a set of ideas that have seized the imagination of senior education leaders faced with the seemingly intractable problems, inadequacies and failures of their existing systems.

These leaders have been systematically and energetically applying the lessons of school improvement to achieve school reform. But while many of their efforts have been rewarded to some degree, the dividends are insufficient. The GELP community believes that the current system of schooling, developed in the age of industrialization, is inadequate for the learning needs of evolving knowledge economies and the dynamic conditions of the new century.

GELP jurisdictions further agree that what is urgently needed is system transformation. However, the implications of this have not been fully understood or accepted. GELP has developed a critique, partly through analyses of existing systems, but also by widening the lens to learn from examples of powerful innovation in other sectors that have transformed people's lives. A transformed system:
• aims to provide equitable access to higher order capabilities, elsewhere called 21st century skills;
• is achieved through holistic transformation because the system is complex and interdependent;
• is characterized by a transfer of power and ownership from teachers to learners in new models of learning, or 21st century pedagogies;
• is accelerated by collaborative learning technologies.

These are the outcomes that we have termed Education 3.0. [22]

LEADING TRANSFORMATION FOR REAL: UNDERSTANDING AND MANAGING RISK

Change is happening at rapidly accelerating speed across GELP jurisdictions. But system leaders in GELP realize that it is by no means inevitable that transformation will unfold in ways most conducive to the full expression of Education 3.0.

There is a need to get ahead of these forces, to shape them so that they contribute positively toward a learning system and a learning society, not a system of fragmented parts where new forms of learning remain in discrete clusters for the benefit of the few. The core challenge for jurisdictions is how to encourage entrepreneurship, innovation and new entrants in education without the state withdrawing from the innovation space entirely and leaving it to non-state providers. Chapter 2 argues that "government as platform" is a powerful way to enable the emergence of a vibrant and equitable *Learning Ecosystem* and takes a look at the Finnish strategy for developing new partnerships.
At least four other risks have been explicitly identified and articulated in GELP:

Tech for tech's sake

The rapid propagation of new technologies does not necessarily lead to new pedagogies. There are numerous examples where the adoption of technology resulted in technology-enabled 20th century pedagogy, where the conversion of textbook to netbook has merely changed the mode of delivery. The influence of technology should be much broader and more profound than this. It includes students' expectations of media ubiquity; the diverse settings in which learning can take place; new pedagogical and assessment tools and methods to ensure their quality; the potential and need for data interoperability; and investments to build teacher capabilities.

More does not always mean better

Curriculum materials and assessments produced by for-profit providers need to be of high quality to avoid the possibility of proliferation without increased sophistication. This requires agreement around the alignment, utility and efficacy of teaching and learning resources: Do they support the goals of Education 3.0? Can teachers and students use them effectively? And do they have a measurable impact on student learning?

Underplaying the importance of values

The need to recognize the functions of school beyond the "academic"—to build culture, values and societal fabric—requires situating these functions within the wider learning society.

The world faces global challenges, which require global solutions. These interconnected global challenges call for far-reaching changes in how we think and act for the dignity of fellow human beings. It is not enough for education to produce individuals who can read, write and count. Education must be transformative and bring shared values to life... It must give people the understanding, skills and values they need to cooperate in resolving the interconnected challenges of the 21st century.[23]

UN Secretary-General's Global Initiative on Education

Sacrificing equity

The increasing privatization of education raises questions of equality and concerns about producing at scale inferior, second-class education for the poorest. Avoiding this relies in part on systems ensuring the spread and diffusion of innovations in learning.

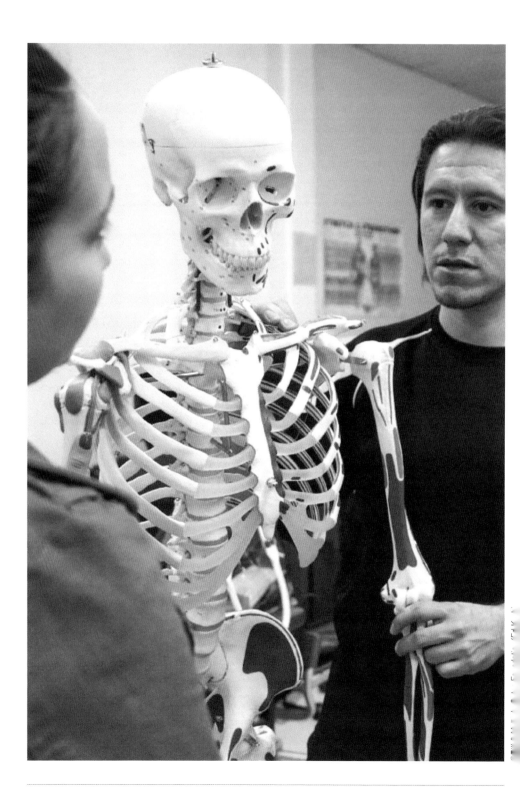

Without genuine change at the micro-level of learning, change efforts at the meso levels of entire organizations and the macro level of education systems will not be reaching learners themselves... There is now a vast research body showing that learning environments can be sustained and disseminated most effectively if they do not work in isolation but are connected to professional learning communities or wider networks with a clear focus on improving learning.[24]

OECD

By working and learning together in a community, system leaders in GELP are exploring with honesty and rigor the extent and effects of these and other risks in their contexts. And they are learning to mitigate these risks through the development of their own discourse and practice and through the use of tools and frameworks, modelled at GELP gatherings, that system leaders take "back to base."

Chapter 5, *Pathways to Possibilities*, explores how teams of system leaders in GELP are developing and using "roadmaps" to plan, test and build support for their transformational journeys. The roadmaps and the tools that help generate them are proving invaluable in conceptualizing, communicating and tackling the practical challenges that arise in bringing transformational ideas and processes to life.

The roadmap continues to guide the team's current work and direction and to discipline its strategic activity, as well as guiding the work of each agency. It assists the team to effectively manage relationships at every level of the education system and to revise strategies in response to changing circumstances.

Future work is expected to focus on sourcing and applying tools and approaches needed for disciplined innovation, and also on development of metrics and methods to best assess schools' and systems' progress and performance.

The roadmap also helps the Australian team to influence the authorizing environment; to promote its vision on the national agenda; and to influence national policy development and implementation within a challenging federal environment.[25]

Susan Mann, GELP Australia

THE FUTURE IS ALREADY HERE—IN POCKETS

As Chapter 3, *Shifting Horizons*, observes, there are exceptional examples of system and school-led innovation, evolving technology-enabled pedagogy, personalized learning and performance-driven transformation occurring in every country around the world. But these innovations are unevenly distributed, largely happening in clusters and at the fringes of systems. They often arise from necessity or freedoms that do not exist in the mainstream.

WE HAVE MANY "BEAUTIFUL EXCEPTIONS" OF INNOVATIVE TEACHING AND LEARNING PROJECTS IN FINLAND. UNFORTUNATELY, THESE INNOVATIVE PROJECTS ARE NOT SCALED UP THROUGHOUT THE COUNTRY. THIS IS CLEARLY A LEADERSHIP CHALLENGE.[26]

Finland presentation, GELP Global Event in Helsinki, 2012

While existing systems are undeniably under stress, a fully operational 21st century education system does not now exist anywhere. But clues on how to reach this new landscape of learning are abundant, backed up by the practical lessons of GELP.

Chapter 4, *Beyond the Fragments*, explores precisely why it is so hard to scale and diffuse exemplary models and practice throughout an entire system and how jurisdictions are tackling this tough challenge.

SO WHAT NOW? THE IMPLEMENTATION AGENDA

Having thoroughly understood the nature of the challenge and developed a coherent and actionable vision for what a transformed system might look like, the question becomes, what do we do about it? As system leaders move into the most exciting phase of GELP's work, they are focusing more and more on identifying and overcoming challenges to implementation. GELP teams are generating important new insights about the real and difficult work of bringing Education 3.0 alive.

They are finding it requires:

A systemic, radical and adaptive innovation strategy

Systemic and radical innovation in education and learning is needed, backed up by an innovation strategy that includes diversity of practices, organizations, platforms and movements at scale. This must include opening up the system to a mix of improvement, supplementation, reinvention and new paradigms for providing learning.

A broader and inclusive dialogue

The new and emerging nature of the world of work requires a much broader conversation, including further and higher education, vocational education, the world of work and communities. Governments often divide education systems into "schools," "universities" and "everything else." These distinctions need to be broken down and combined and their purposes reframed.

Systematic culture change

The tipping point for change remains a shift in "public" culture, thinking and conceptions of education's form and purpose. This can happen through building learning communities—between schools and their communities, between learners

and educators and among educator networks. It requires acknowledging the power of learners and educators to be agents of change, rather than groups in need of convincing.

New forms of system leadership

The GELP community benefits from experts in education and system leadership, including support from some of the world's leading thinkers on system and leadership change. Nevertheless it has struggled to find models or frameworks for understanding and developing leadership equal to the task of transformation. Chapter 6, *Movers and Shapers*, explores why this might be the case and offers an analysis of what the leadership job of system transformation requires.

In summary, new forms of leadership must balance a "split-screen" that pays attention to improvement on the one hand and transformation on the other, while navigating the politics of education in the interest of learners. Leadership for innovation must embrace the experimental and anticipate what's next, leading both on the edge of improvement and the emerging ecosystem of learning. Practically, this requires forming partnerships and coalitions of teams of key education thinkers, leaders and world-class organizations determined to transform education. [27]

THE PROMISE OF THE FUTURE

The parameters of a new learning system are emerging. This book offers not just a compelling case for change but real, compelling practice around the world.

There is evidence that the future is already here—from the journey of the GELP jurisdictions so far, to the emerging roadmaps for how systems are designing and implementing participatory learning practices in learning organizations and on learning platforms.

Education 3.0 is galvanizing professionals, politicians, parents, young people, companies, non-profits and social entrepreneurs who recognize that learning is everybody's business.

A new cadre of system leaders is shaping increasingly connected, self-generating learning systems in various parts of the world. But it has only just begun. It will take an on-going commitment to a process of innovation and entrepreneurship if we are to find new ways to meet the needs of our citizens—global citizens—in life and work.

NOTES AND SOURCES

[1] Ericsson. (October 2012). The Future of Learning. http://www.youtube.com/watch?v=quYDkuD4dMU

[2] Cisco. (2010). The Learning Society. http://gelponline.org/resources/learning-society

[3] Leadbeater, C., and Wong, A., (2010). Learning from the Extremes. Cisco. http://gelponline.org/resources/learning-extremes

[4] Hannon, V., Patton, A., and Temperley, J. (2011). Developing an Innovation Ecosystem for Education http://gelponline.org/resources/developing-innovation-ecosystem-education

[5] Cisco. (2008). Equipping Every Learner for the 21st Century. http://gelponline.org/resources/equipping-every-learner-21st-century

[6] Why WISE? World Innovation Summit for Education. http://www.wise-qatar.org/content/wise-initiative

[7] See Leadbeater, C. (2008). What's Next? 21 Ideas for 21st Century Learning. http://goo.gl/L5z0g

[8] See Zhao, Y. (2012). World Class Learners: Educating Creative and Entrepreneurial Students http://goo.gl/4Rje7

[9] zhaolcarning.com/world-class-learners my new book/about/

[10] www.att.com/gen/corporate-citizenship?pid=17922

[11] www.telstra.com.au/business-enterprise/download/document/business-education-whitepaper-2011.pdf

[12] www.oecd.org/site/eduilebanff/ceriinnovativelearningenvironmentsile.htm

[13] See World Bank. (April 2012). Learning for All. http://goo.gl/31CHh

[14] See Hannon, V., Gillinson, S., and Shanks, L. (2012). Learning a Living: Radical Innovation in Education for Work. (Bloomsbury). http://www.wise-qatar.org/2012-wise-book

[15] www.globaleducationfirst.org/index.html

[16] gordonandsarahbrown.com/category/education-for-all/

[17] See Brown, G. Delivering on the promise, building opportunity. http://goo.gl/8i4H2 and Education for All: beating poverty, unlocking prosperity. http://goo.gl/GL9zd

[18] http://siteresources.worldbank.org/EDUCATION/Resources/ESSU/EducationStrategyUpdate_April2012.pdf

[19] http://www.bigpicture.org/category/schools/

[20] Schleicher, A. (November 2011). Building a High-Quality Teaching Profession: Lessons from around the World. (OECD Publishing). http://dx.doi.org/10.1787/9789264113046-en

[21] http://at21st centurys.org/index.php/about/what-are-21st-century-skills/

[22] Cisco. (2008). Equipping Every Learner for the 21st Century. http://gelponline.org/resources/equipping-every-learner-21st-century

[23] http://www.globaleducationfirst.org/220.htm

[24] OECD. (2011). Innovative Learning Environments, International Conference on Innovative Learning Environments. Innovations in the Ile Project: A Preliminary Synthesis. www.oecd.org/site/eduilebanff/48834621.pdf

[25] Quoted in Miller, R., (2013). Evaluating GELP: Towards Making Experimentalist Leadership Practical. Global Education Leaders' Program.

[26] Finland Presentation. (2012). GELP Global Event, Helsinki.

[27] Miller, R., (2013). Evaluating GELP: Towards Making Experimentalist Leadership Practical. Global Education Leaders' Program.

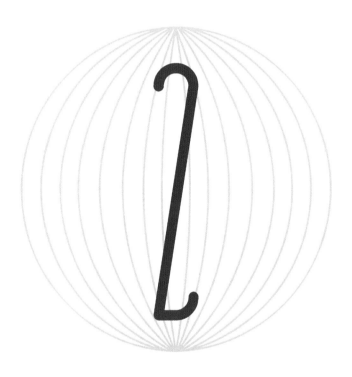

TOWARD A LEARNING ECOSYSTEM: NEW PLAYERS, NEW PARTNERSHIPS

The debate around the nature of Education 3.0 includes who gets to play in the game, with big implications for current players in the system, emerging players and those who do not yet play but want and need to. We are witnessing an unprecedented opening up of learning opportunities—which is welcome and overdue.

For too long education has been a "secret garden," with closed groups determining process and content, and access to quality education limited to the few. Enabled by digital technologies and inspired by new models of social change, learning systems are en route to becoming more like ecosystems: diverse, interdependent, fluid and crucially requiring a fostering platform on which to evolve and grow. To appreciate the potential of this vision we first need to understand the rapid shift that has taken place in who provides education and its potential as a key source of further innovation.

REDEFINING "SYSTEM"

Early exemplars hint at the practices, environments and methods of learning that a transformed system could create. Chapter 3, *Shifting Horizons*, explores some of these examples. But they are only examples. The explosion of learning apps and new devices can enable still undeveloped ways of learning. Practitioners are in the midst of experimenting with these new tools to evolve new pedagogies—

fundamentally new learning designs—and these are still emerging. But nowhere has yet recognized fully the *systemic* dimension of the needed change.

In the modern world, full access for all citizens to coherent, powerful learning opportunities depends on a complex system of people, infrastructure, finance, technologies and regulatory frameworks. These are interrelated. We cannot effectively transform the system by addressing only one or two dimensions. The focus of GELP has been to work with system leaders to help them become innovative *systems* thinkers and actors.

However, GELP recognizes the limitations of working exclusively with conventional "system leaders." Reform efforts of the past 20 years have done just that, on the premise that change is a task for educational professionals, driven by politicians through education bureaucracies. Other players have bit parts and walk-on roles. The "system" has meant the vertical management-and-funding from jurisdictional government through district to school to classroom. This established system seems concretized and impermeable, yet it was assembled by 19th century reformers from the fragments created by social entrepreneurs (religious and philanthropic innovators).[28]

Transformation in the public sector cannot happen in a vacuum; it happens at the nexus of policy, research, capital, practice and social movements (or behavior change). [29] In short, as learning becomes substantially more important to every part of global society, the whole approach to how it is conceived, organized, funded and nurtured must be reengineered.

The drivers for transformation stem from a wide range of sources and have implications across all segments of society. A broad range of players are demanding more relevant, adaptive and value-based learning systems. Yet few of these actors, despite their stakes in the system, have managed to effect or influence change. The realization of a *learning society* [30] —which is rhetorically what every nation now aspires to—depends upon a different, much more inclusive concept of system.

New conditions now combine to compel us to think in terms of a *learning ecosystem*. An ecosystem is defined [31] as "the complex of a community of organisms and its environment functioning as an ecological unit." The application of this biological metaphor to learning is intended to convey the fluid and dynamic interdependence of diverse constituents, maintained by a supportive infrastructure. It marks a shift from the closed, institutionally bound conception of the 20th century. The (literal) ecosystem of the coral reef is illuminating. Darwin's exploration of this phenomenon revealed that the physical platform (created by the skeletons of millions of soft polyps) created a habitat within which literally millions of other species could co-exist and flourish. While within it there is competition for resources, species also collaborate, with mutually supportive outcomes. [32]

To rethink education as a learning ecosystem will entail reviewing how it is governed and provided. This will require: [33]
• a new form of stewardship from a coalition of governments, businesses, nongovernmental organizations and social investors who together bring legitimacy, innovation and resources. The membership of this movement will vary, but it must deliver a clear articulation of its collective purpose and goals and be open to an ever-expanding group of supporters, innovators and funders;
• a mixture of learning providers—public, private and third sector organizations and individuals who provide content, learning opportunities and great pedagogy to learners of all ages. To drive innovation, a learning society must actively encourage new entrants and not allow monopolies to persist;
• telecom and network providers (supported by governments) who help ensure access to a shared learning infrastructure—the roads and rails of the learning society. Making learning easy to access is fundamental to encouraging uptake and means providing seamless, high-quality, low-cost (preferably no-cost) connectivity at home, at work, on the move and in public spaces; and
• a flourishing, mature market of educational resources at the disposal of enabled and informed purchasers (involving families and learners, not just institutions).

LEARNING FROM SOCIAL INNOVATION

In the last decade a new model of social change has taken root, in which social innovation is not planned and strategized exclusively by governments but rather arises in myriad fluid forms, involving often unlikely new players and partners. Writers such as Clay Shirky, Stephen Johnson, Charles Leadbeater, Richard Florida and Clay Christensen[34] have analysed and illustrated how fundamental social changes have come about. How people access learning is no different. Governments may be one player in a rapidly developing ecosystem, but few have adapted themselves purposely and productively to this role. Geoff Mulgan argues that while systemic innovation is much harder to orchestrate than, say, product innovation, still:

in all these cases... [Karelia, Finland and Fredericia, Denmark in public health; Singapore in e-government; Germany in renewable energy; the Reggio Emilia approach to early childhood in Italy] individuals and groups helped shape the new system as an idea before it became a reality. In some—like the post-war economic system—tiny numbers of people played a decisive role. All systems are to some extent emergent—none precisely follow anyone's blueprint. But it can be misleading to see everything as "emergent," without any conscious shaping.[35]

While current system leaders need a new appreciation of the emergent learning ecosystem of which they are a part, they can also play a vital role in shaping and accelerating it for the public good.

WHO ARE THE NEW PLAYERS?

A vibrant and dynamic learning ecosystem will comprise new coalitions for stewardship, bringing innovation and resources and also a new mix of providers, creating new modes and opportunities for learning. In the last 5 years, the education landscape has become crowded with new players from all sectors evolving new roles for themselves. Who are they?

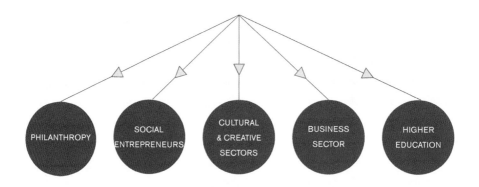

Philanthropy is now a major driver of innovation in education, arguably providing the key resources for experimentation and change that governments have been loathe (or unable) to do. This is true both in emergent and developed economies. In the former, UNESCO shows [36] how billions of dollars now flow from foundations in support of the Millennium Development Goals (Education for All) in some of the poorest countries in the world. In India, the Azim Premji Foundation,[37] the Bharti Foundation[38] and the Shiv Nadar Foundation,[39] have reached many millions of children, principally in under-served rural areas. Similarly the Tanoto Foundation[40] in Indonesia, the Hüsnü M. Özye in Foundation[41] in Turkey, and the foundation of Carlos Slim Helú[42] in Mexico have become major players. And UNESCO reports that US Fortune 500 companies gave philanthropic contributions to education in developing countries projected at nearly $500 million annually; 70% in the form of cash support. Within the United States, according to Giving USA, Americans donated $39 billion to education organizations in 2011. This sum made education the second largest philanthropic sector of the year with 13% of total giving. Between 2006 and 2010, the top fifteen philanthropic organizations gave a total of $7,376 million to education.[43] Aside from the volumes involved, the Bill & Melinda Gates Foundation, Hewlett, and Macarthur Foundations arguably provide the most significant engines for innovation in education impacting the system. In the UK, foundations such as the Paul Hamlyn Trust, NESTA and Esmee Fairburn provide the seed funding for significant experimentation.

Social Entrepreneurs are one of the key sources of ideas and innovation in learning today. The non-profit sector has exploded with activity. BRAC,[44] the largest social enterprise, reaches 110 million children worldwide through a holistic approach that combines microfinance, education, healthcare, legal services and community empowerment. At the other end of the spectrum, one-person, value-driven, online enterprises are making a radical difference. It is impossible to quantify this sector; it's growing so rapidly. It is especially inspiring that it frequently involves young, socially conscious entrepreneurs (sometimes teachers) who are values driven, want to make a tangible difference to their societies and see learning as the critical space in which to do so.[45] This might involve working with young people at risk or already in detention; the particularly gifted or artistically inspired; the disengaged or disconnected; or those with a strong community orientation, who find little or nothing in school to engage or enable their passion. These "models from the margins" can be the source of exciting pedagogical innovation, which in due course will influence the old school-bound factory-style approach. Social

entrepreneurs are behind some of the most innovative US charter schools, and they are establishing free schools in the UK intentionally to inhabit the space for innovation.

The Cultural and Creative Sectors have become more self-consciously engaged with learning. Programs like *Creative Partnerships* in the UK brought the expertise and perspectives of the creative sector in direct and formal engagement with schools to catalyse innovation. You also see this in individual localities, such as Kuopio in Finland, where a city has leveraged all its cultural and creative resources to develop schools as cultural communities. And many great cultural assets, such as the Smithsonian in Washington, the Melbourne Museum Victoria in Australia and the Royal Shakespeare Company in the UK are re-assessing and ramping up their learning offerings, whether virtual or "real world." Naturally there are now multitudes of opportunities for cultural and creative learning directly online.[46]

The Business Sector also has become a major part of the education landscape. Private schools are of course nothing new. However, in many jurisdictions businesses are now able to enter into the market by opening chains of schools (academies in the UK, charters in the US, etc.). And businesses are providing low-cost private schools in much the same way churches historically have in places like Australia. Pearson leads the way in this space,[47] now running low-cost private schools across Africa, Asia and South America.

The scantiest internet search will uncover scores of online providers of a myriad of learning services, aimed at every market segment from prospective parents to students, families, teachers and school leaders. And their offerings cover every aspect of learning, from content to process, pedagogy and systems management. NewsCorp's Amplify,[48] led by Joel Klein—formerly the Chancellor of New York City's Public Schools—exemplifies the range of offerings. It will focus on curriculum content, new delivery systems (in partnership with AT&T) and learning analytics. The challenge for the learner, of whatever age or stage, is not so much finding what you want, but being confident of its quality.

Other forms of business engagement should not be overlooked. For example, the innovative non-profit Big Picture Learning relies on heavily engaged business partners to realize its disruptive learning model. Big Picture's learning design incorporates two day per week internships for students in a range of businesses and community organizations. It is impossible to implement this with the level of success these schools do without the sustained active commitment of business.[49]

Higher education. The creation of MOOCs (Massive Open Online Courses) has just begun to leverage the vast resources of higher education in the service of a transformed system. In the United States millions of school students are now taking college-level courses, and schools themselves are now smudging the too-rigid institutional boundaries and are designing learning opportunities spanning college and school.[50] Meanwhile, online organizations are offering matching services to learners seeking to navigate their way through the myriad of opportunities.[51]

HOW SHOULD THIS EXPANSION BE VIEWED?

It is not hard to find voices decrying this explosion of providers, funders and innovators in education. In most cases the criticism springs from the view that education is a public good and therefore should be publicly provided; that the profit motive should have no place in the provision of public services; that only public (tax)-funded and provided schools can be relied upon to guarantee quality and equity; and that the involvement of business is a ruse to drive down the pay and conditions of professional educators. It is hard to see how this argument can be sustained given that:

• other services—such as shelter or food—are equally "public goods," essential to the conduct of civilised life; yet no one argues these days that they should be wholly funded and provided by the state;

• total state monopolies thus far have not done a great job providing universal high quality learning or producing equitable outcomes (save in those instances where the societies are already fundamentally equal, such as in the Nordic countries).

So far, this has been a very confused public debate, as Michael Horn points out in his 2011 paper on the role of the private sector.[52] Business is already deeply involved in many aspects of learning (textbooks, exams, etc.) and an extension of these roles should be properly debated and assessed. The key is framing the right "ask" and offer, and ensuring the right controls are in place. Businesses are no more inherently evil than non-profits or state-run institutions are always efficient, effective and incorruptible.

In any case, this horse has certainly bolted. The demand side—learners—are voting with their feet, and will without question become increasingly empowered as a welter of new opportunities—online, face-to-face and blended—become available to them.[53] The question then becomes: How are system leaders, especially those committed to the transformation of the system for the wider public good, to respond and react?

These developments should in general be welcomed, not fought. But there is much that innovative leaders within current systems can do, from their strategic standpoint, to further their particular commitment to equity and the deepest values in education. There is now a growing literature on how the public, private and non-profit sectors can work together to advance education innovation.[54] Not least, for businesses and other new providers to do a good job in providing high quality educational services and tools, they need collaboration between the public sector and research institutions, including knowledge of innovative pedagogies and learning theories. A reciprocal relationship is important and necessary.

ASSESSING THE LOCAL ECOSYSTEM

One important starting point is to have an overview, within a coherent conceptual framework, of current activity within jurisdictions. GELP has developed a tool to help leaders map and assess initiatives within their systems. The ecosystem heuristic grid is one way to assess the diversity of providers and innovative drive within a system. GELP evolved this tool from two antecedents: first, the Innovation Grid proposed by Leadbeater and Wong in Learning from the Extremes;[55] and second, from a model developed in work focused on radical efficiency in public services by Innovation Unit.[56]

The ecosystem grid[57]

The theory underpinning this grid is that innovation initiatives can be "mapped" according to how and where they situate learning (formal/informal), and also by the nature of the provider. Scanning innovation in education across many examples, we have found that initiatives located in the top left quadrant are focused on "school improvement" techniques, within classrooms, with the aims and metrics of the existing system intact. By contrast, initiatives found in the bottom right quadrant tend to be directed at fundamentally new models, capable of disrupting our concepts of provision. Examples in this space might include the well-known *Hole in the Wall* program,[58] which places computers in poor communities in India and internationally to encourage children to engage in self-led, collaborative, play-based learning, and many of the examples falling under the Blended Learning rubric[59] well described by the Innosight Institute. Of course these are inductively arrived at. The model is merely a heuristic; just one way of thinking about these phenomena. It is not normative or prescriptive; not *all* new entrants and entrepreneurs are *necessarily* or automatically innovative—one can readily think of examples that are highly traditional. Additionally, some existing providers—creative teachers in established schools—may be involved in reinventing schools, although we have yet to come across any who are creating new paradigms. This is consistent with the arguments advanced by writers such as Clayton Christensen,[60] who sees new entrants as the principle source of radical and disruptive innovation, but it may not always remain the case.

Overlaid onto these spaces is the idea of the emergence of game changers: radical shifts and new factors that dramatically influence systems and practices in learning. Our research indicates that in most contexts these are:
• the transfer of ownership to the learner; and
• the optimal use of powerful digital technologies.[61]

Using the grid, system leaders can map the range of known initiatives in the appropriate spaces and reflect on the extent to which systems leverage these powerful new players and dimensions through enabling conditions, policy development, resource decisions and so on.

The purpose is not to suggest that all innovation should reside in, or migrate to, the bottom right quadrant. The tasks of improving the existing system must proceed simultaneously with seeding and developing the new paradigm. Hence the concept of ecosystem: Are there exemplars of all forms of innovation to be found? And is the system benefiting from this diversity by knowledge exchange between the models?

System leaders in GELP have exploited this tool in different ways. Most jurisdictions in the program have used the tool firstly as an analytic aid to explore their own understandings of innovation exemplars from around the world; it is an aid to thinking clearly. What exactly is going on in the example? What are its strengths? Participants also use the grid to assess the state of play within their jurisdictions: What examples fall into the four quadrants? How densely or evenly are they distributed? What is the relationship, if any, between examples across the quadrants? It is a tool to think about the state of play of innovation within the jurisdiction.

In Finland, for example, team members from The Finnish Board of Education worked with colleagues from the University of Helsinki to plot the wide variety of innovation initiatives within the education sector, which are a marked feature of the Finnish system. In 2012 the team conducted a pilot to identify and plot the range. This is how the Finnish grid looked:

The Finnish ecosystem grid

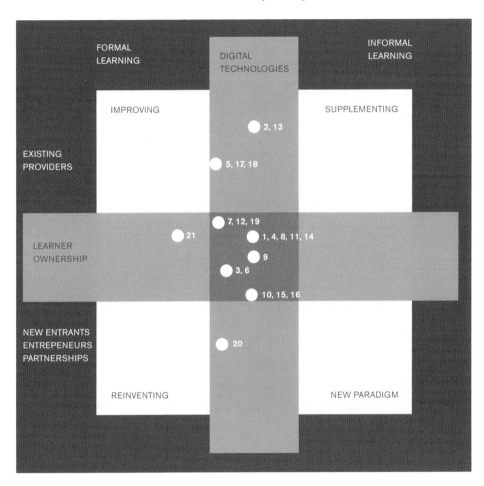

1: On the Move!
2: Culture Path Program Kuopio
3: Fiskars Model
4: PaikkaOppi
5: Problem-based teaching and learning online
6: UBIKO - School cells as inspiring pedagogical spaces in support of learning
7: Media play as a learning environment in pre-primary and initial education
8: Tulevaisuuden oppimismenetelmät ja −ympäristöt
9: AVO − Avoimet verkostot oppimiseen
10: Kylä kaupungissa
11: Visci Research Project

12: KivaKoulu
13: Sormet - Arjen oppimis- kokemukset sulautuvissa oppimisympäristöissä
14: Agents
15: eOppiminen.fi
16: In search of mobile learning
17: School 3.1
18: Kulkuri ('Tramp') − online school for expatriate children 19: Piloting and dissemination of Dream School services: tablet computers and user-oriented educational games
20: Momaths
21: Seasons of learning in the outdoor school

The lessons the team drew from their research included:
• it helped them "see the forest from the trees"; there was felt to be an insufficiency of action in the informal sector;
• "beautiful exceptions" were not spreading and diffusing; and
• more should be done to explore the possibilities of public-private partnerships and multi-professional collaboration.[62]

The innovation grid gave these system leaders a wider lens with which to view and assess their system in order to shape their strategy and action. One GELP member (deeply involved in teacher preparation) from South Korea observed:
One of the big lessons I learnt from the GELP approach is (the importance of) informal education. 70% of what kids learn is from informal education. But even though it's very important, teacher training does not see it. So I just became a CEO of an entrepreneurial company for education service, a company to provide training for informal education. We create and develop curriculum materials for informal education. And we do promotion and communication activity.[63]

Professor OkHwa Lee, GELP South Korea

IMPLICATIONS FOR THE ROLE OF GOVERNMENT

Recognizing the new landscape—the ecosystem—within which learning occurs has important implications for system leaders, both professional and political. Just as the roles of learner and teacher are evolving, so must the roles of those who steward publicly funded systems.

Governments around the world fulfil a wide range of functions in relation to education that vary according to history, culture and ideology. In some nations with emergent economies, governments struggle with issues of scale and reach, unable to satisfy basic needs of access and quality, and a wide variety of other providers have sprung up. Government capacity to regulate or assure the quality of these can be as weak as its power to provide. Elsewhere, government's powerfully dominant role in education is being contested increasingly. In the UK political parties have of late warmed to the notion of a shifting government role and a wider diversity of providers. In the US, the perennial debate between the proponents of "big" and "small" government is alive and well.

Tim O'Reilly,[64] who has written extensively on the theme of government as platform, argues that absorbing the lessons from innovation in technology can resolve this sterile debate between "big" and "small" government; between government as the (near) monopoly provider and a totally privatized market solution. His vision is one in which government provides appropriate platforms for many providers and players to contribute and interact in vibrant collaboration/competition. While he writes mainly about the digital environment, some of that thinking applies to the broader questions of education.

Platforms have a key economic role because they are engines of innovation; they make us think differently about the nature of products and services. Instead of limited products or services with pre-determined uses, they become alive, fuelled by continuous innovation brought about by third-parties. The perfect exemplar is that of Apple's iTunes store (the platform) and the ensuing explosion of App products by third parties.

A platform role does not entail a less complex one, stripped-down to its bare essentials. Crucially, it does not entail government withdrawing completely and letting the market prevail. It requires a fostering and nurturing of both the conditions for innovation and the innovations themselves. There are four roles that only government can, and should, perform:
• vision and leadership, democratically legitimated;
• ensuring fundamental entitlements;
• the promotion and assurance of equity; and
• safety and safeguarding.

Add to these a new set of roles, focused specifically on fostering innovation through creating the conditions in which it might flourish. Such conditions include:
1. an inspiring vision for lifelong and engaged learning, with aims beyond personal wealth and economic competitiveness;
2. low barriers of entry for new providers;
3. incentives for social enterprises, businesses, creative and cultural organizations, user groups, philanthropists and non-government organizations to become more actively engaged in the design, provision and support of learning opportunities for children and people of all ages;
4. freedom for merger and de-merger activity;
5. incentivizing student-led curriculum development;
6. greater transparency for learners about the range of opportunities available;

7. coalition building; and

8. investment in, and encouragement for, disciplined "innovation zones"—and then in enabling the diffusion of successful models and practices.

Under this model, government is a *convener and enabler, a broker and a facilitator* - as well as the democratically elected or appointed body with a mandate to set out the overall direction of the system.

From a different perspective, but with an equally challenging intervention, writers such as Stears and Mulgan[65] argue that there has been too little fresh discussion of the purpose and role of the state in general—and public services in particular. They argue that, in some western countries, there is a growing consensus on the need for human relationships to be given greater priority as a goal of policy and in the design and operation of public services. This challenges a strict adherence to egalitarian goals and state-led agency above all others. In some contexts, the fear that any variation or contingency in service provision would produce unacceptable inequalities has driven a bias towards centralization and standardization that sapped professional creativity and local mobilization. For such writers, a move away from "the delivery state" to "the relational state" is what is needed.

This may seem a very western-oriented debate. Within GELP, there are jurisdictions with widely diverse forms and traditions of government and concepts about the role of the state, and these are unlikely to change anytime soon. Nevertheless, the demands of what Al Gore has called "Earth Inc"[66] (That is, the emergence of a deeply interconnected global economy that increasingly operates *as a fully integrated holistic entity*) concentrates the minds of governments who recognize they desperately need creative innovative learners—and that they may need to rethink their role in *their* ecosystem if that goal is to be achieved.

Actively promoting a learning ecosystem entails that system leaders rethink the role of government and its agencies in the whole. System leaders in GELP certainly recognize the need for some re-assessment. A leader from GELP British Columbia, Canada remarked:

… it's part of the changing relationship with the state and the people. So the role of the state is as much as a broker as a driver. An organization that looks in and provides some assessment and some opinions on how things are going as opposed to the driver of everything.[67]

And a member of the GELP Australia team observed:

The key is articulating the vision for change, but not owning the vision... (this) helps us to understand ourselves as a platform, rather than individual providers. That's taking people a lot of time to get how they work, and how they work with stakeholders. But that's been a direct effect for me—repositioning us.[68]

System leaders should see themselves as assisting the evolution of a broader ecology of learning that is lifelong and life-wide, supported by myriad providers and vendors. This development should be welcomed, not resisted; it will provide the energy, investment and disruptive innovation needed for large-scale, sustainable transformation. The balance of learning methods, practices and providers will necessarily vary in differing cultural traditions. However, in rethinking their role in such an ecosystem, governments should have regard to some key questions central to effecting long-lasting change:

• What is it that they, and only they, can and should do in the new environment?

• Should a broader notion of what counts as "the system" of education be advanced?

• Are entitlement and equity the key values of "the system," and how are they to be promoted and safeguarded in the new world of learning?

• What can they do further to energize the new ecosystem, in particular to enable new sources of innovation?

• And when these arise, how can they intentionally assist their diffusion across "the system," so that all learners have access to the best that is emerging?

Fundamental to examining these questions and their implications is a re-evaluation of the principles, ethics and purposes behind the work as a whole. To begin asking how to achieve the learning we want, we must first ask: What is education *for*?

NOTES AND SOURCES

[28] See Leadbeater, C. (2013). The Systems Innovator. Nesta. www.nesta.org.uk/library/documents/Systemsinnovationv8.pdf

[29] See Mulgan, G., and Leadbeater, C. (2008). Innovation for the Public Good. (Series). Nesta. http://bellwethereducation.org/innovation-for-the-public-good/

[30] Cisco. (2010).The Learning Society. gelponline.org/resources/learning-society

[31] www.merriam-webster.com/dictionary/ecosystem

[32] Darwin, C. (1842). The Structure and Distribution of Coral Reefs. http://darwin-online.org.uk/converted/published/1842_Coral_F271/1842_Coral_F271.html

[33] Cisco. (2010).The Learning Society. gelponline.org/resources/learning-society

[34] See, for example, Shirky, C. (2008). Here Comes Everybody: The Power of Organizing Without Organizations. (Allen Lane);

Johnson, S. (2012). Future Perfect: The Case for Progress in a Networked Age. (Riverhead);

Florida, R. (2002). The Rise of the Creative Class. (Basic Books);

Christensen, C. (1997). The Innovator's Dilemma. (Harvard Business School Press); and Christensen, Johnson, C. W. and Horne, M. (2008). Disrupting the Class: How Disruptive Innovation Will Change the Way the World Learns. (McGraw Hill); for Charles Leadbeater's work see http://www.charlesleadbeater.net/

[35] Mulgan, G. (2013). Joined Up Innovation. Nesta. www.nesta.org.uk/library/documents/Systemsinnovationv8.pdf

[36] van Fleet, J. (2012). Private Philanthropy & Social Investments in Support of Education for All. UNESCO. http://unesdoc.unesco.org/images/0021/002179/217920e.pdf

[37] http://www.azimpremjifoundation.org/

[38] http://www.bhartifoundation.org

[39] http://www.shivnadarfoundation.org/

[40] http://www.tanotofoundation.org/

[41] http://www.husnuozyeginvakfi.org.tr/

[42] http://www.carlosslim.com

[43] http://foundationcenter.org/findfunders/statistics/

[44] http://www.brac.net/

[45] See, for example, Israel. http://www.826national.org/once-upon-a-school/656/international-collaboration

[46] See, for example, http://826valencia.org/

[47] http://www.affordable-learning.com

[48] http://amplify.com/

[49] See the Big Picture case study in Hannon, V., Gillinson, S., and Shanks, L. (2013). Learning a Living: Radical Innovation in Education for Work. (Bloomsbury), pp. 80-86.

[50] Number and percentage of public high school graduates taking dual credit; 2005 and 2009, U.S. Digest of Education Statistics. http://nces.ed.gov/programs/digest/d11/tables/dt11_163. asp; update on figures in 2012: http://www.politifact.com/truth-o-meter/promises/obameter/ promise/261/increase-the-number-of-high-school-students-taking/. For a model that blends school, college and work boundaries, see College Unbound. http://collegeunbound.org/

[51] For one example of such an organization, see http://www.saylor.org/

[52] Horn, M B., (April 2011). Beyond Good and Evil: Understanding the Role of For-Profits in Education through the Theories of Disruptive Innovation. Innosight

[53] See, for example, Innovation Unit. (2012). QA for Educational Resources in the US. Bill & Melinda Gates Foundation.

[54] Petersen, J. and Smith, K. Steering Capital: Optimizing Financial Support for Innovation in Public Education. http://bellwethereducation.org/steering-capital-optimizing-financial-support-for- innovation-in-public-education/

[55] Set out in Leadbeater, C., and Wong, A., (2010). Learning from the Extremes. Cisco. http://gelponline. org/resources/learning-extremes

[56] Gillinson, S., Horne, M. and Baeck, P., (2011). Radical Efficiency: Different, better, lower cost public services. Innovation Unit. www.innovationunit.org/knowledge/our-ideas/radical-efficiency

[57] The provenance of this tool is set out in full in Hannon, V., Patton, A., and Temperley, J. (2011). Developing an Innovation Ecosystem for Education. http://gelponline.org/resources/developing- innovation-ecosystem-education

[58] www.hole-in-the-wall.com/

[59] http://www.innosightinstitute.org/media-room/publications/blended-learning/blended-learning- model-definitions/

[60] Christensen, C. (1997). The Innovator's Dilemma. (Harvard Business School Press); and Christensen, Johnson, C. W. and Horne, M. (2008). Disrupting the Class: How Disruptive Innovation Will Change the

Way the World Learns. (McGraw Hill).

[61] Horn, M J. (2013). As Digital Learning Draws New Users, Transformation Will Occur. http://educationnext.org/as-digital-learning-draws-new-users-transformation-will-occur/

[62] For further detail on the Finnish findings from this pilot, see Professor Kristiina Kumpulainen. we.clients.wiredesign.com/pages/story/introduction/423,527/kristiina_kumpulainen.html

[63] Miller, R., (2013). Evaluating GELP: Towards Making Experimentalist Leadership Practical. Global Education Leaders' Program.

[64] O'Reilly, T. (2010). Government as a Platform. O'Reilly Media. http://ofps.oreilly.com/titles/9780596804350/

[65] Muir, R. and Cooke, G. (2012). The Relational State: How Recognising the Importance of Human Relationships Could Revolutionise the Role of the State. Institute for Public Policy Research. http://www.ippr.org/images/media/files/publication/2012/11/relational-state_Nov2012_9888.pdf

[66] Gore, A. (2013). The Future. (WH Allen).

[67] Miller, R., (2013). Evaluating GELP: Towards Making Experimentalist Leadership Practical. Global Education Leaders' Program.

[68] ibid.

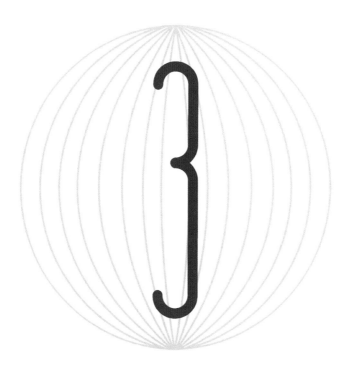

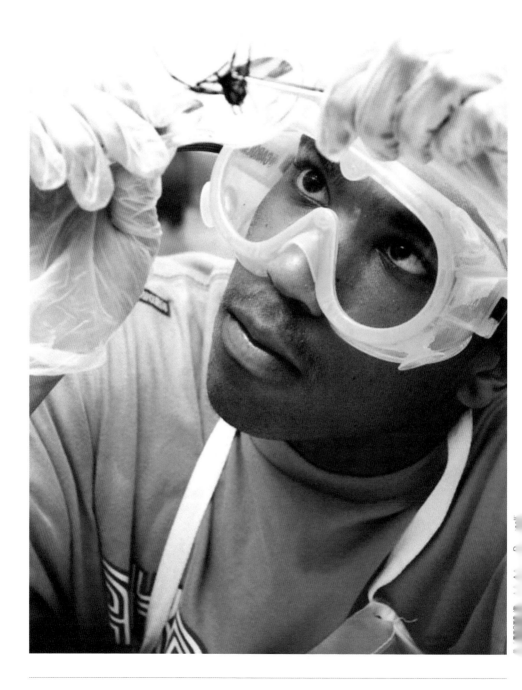

SHIFTING HORIZONS AND EMERGING REALITIES

The future is already here—it's just not evenly distributed.[6]

William Gibson

To transform schooling at scale, we need clear evidence about what works in learning combined with a radical, alternative vision of what's possible.

In short, we need a set of rigorous and bold design principles on which transformation can be built—principles that can drive the redesign of learning and schooling and offer both a framework against which to evaluate and connect new practices and a vehicle to support their spread.

GELP has devised this new design architecture by scanning the emerging international landscape of promising practices and models that now live on the fringes of the existing system, albeit in a dispersed and uncoordinated fashion.

PURPOSES—WHAT IS EDUCATION FOR?

Harold Benjamin's 1939 article *The Sabre-toothed Curriculum*[70] satirized a tribe who introduced sabre-toothed-tiger-scaring-with-fire into the curriculum to meet the present challenges of tribal life beyond school. Many years down the line, with the sabre-toothed tiger threat gone, attempts were made to change the school curriculum, but the proposals were met with, "You must know that there are some eternal verities, and the sabre-toothed curriculum is one of them."

The moral is a simple one: Society evolves and the purposes and processes and content of learning and schooling have to change, too, or it ceases to serve young people or society well.

THE EDUCATOR'S JOB IS NOT TO PREPARE KIDS TO DO WELL IN SCHOOL, BUT TO DO WELL IN LIFE.[71]

Elliot Eisner

Our world—life—has changed, and with it our expectations of education. In 2011 the *Times Educational Supplement* in England initiated an online debate around the purpose of education. The following represent the themes that emerged. Education should:[72]
• promote passion for and engagement in learning;
• grow humanity—empathy and collaborative intent;
• stimulate curiosity, imagination and a futures orientation;
• develop the skills to become confident, independent decision-makers able to shape our future;
• build resilience and introduce the joy of failing forward; and
• induct into different cultures and different worlds.

While the list is not definitive, it is very different from what it might have been twenty or so years ago.

We are now at a point where we must educate our children in what no one knew yesterday, and prepare our schools for what no one knows yet.[73]

Margaret Mead

LEARNING—RESEARCH THAT CAN INFORM DESIGN PRINCIPLES

Much is now known about how people learn. Yet too much of young people's school experience does not fit well with that evidence. Two major works of synthesis—one the largest ever meta-analyses of effect sizes of different education methods, the other a future-oriented study from the OECD—are worth citing in this context.

John Hattie's seminal study of 800 approaches to teaching and learning finds that "feedback" (defined as teacher to student, student to teacher and student to student) has the highest effect size of any intervention, and that "disposition to learn" is among the six highest effect size features.[74]

Students who are actively engaged in learning for deeper understanding are likely to learn more than students that are not so engaged.[75]

The "grand meta-principle," Kathryn Patricia Cross

Note that engagement here is not simply a synonym for motivation. It is more complex. Learners are deeply engaged when they:

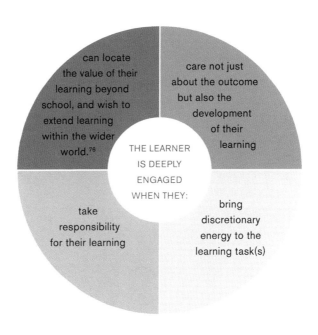

can locate the value of their learning beyond school, and wish to extend learning within the wider world.[76]

care not just about the outcome but also the development of their learning

THE LEARNER IS DEEPLY ENGAGED WHEN THEY:

take responsibility for their learning

bring discretionary energy to the learning task(s)

This deep form of engagement—in the process of learning as well as what is being learnt—was also identified by the OECD in *The Nature of Learning*,[77] which defined an effective learning environment as a place that:

1. Makes learning central, encourages engagement, and where learners increasingly understand themselves as learners;
2. ensures that learning is social and often collaborative;
3. is highly attuned to the learners' motivations and the key role of emotions;
4. is acutely sensitive to individual differences, including in prior knowledge;
5. is demanding for each learner but without excessive overload;
6. uses assessments that are consistent with its aims, with strong emphasis on formative feedback; and
7. promotes horizontal connectedness across activities and subjects, in and out of school.

So, we know that the purposes of education have evolved. We know more about what works. We know what great learning might look like. What we are less clear about, but are starting to form some ideas about in GELP, are the forward-looking principles, rooted in evidence and the purpose of education in the 21st century, which can drive learning design and offer focus, coherence and consistency to system transformation efforts.

LEARNING AT THE MARGINS

Any talk of transforming learning must acknowledge that there have been alternative models of schooling for as long as there have been schools. Ways of learning outside institutions also persist—informal learning, self-directed learning, expeditionary learning[78] and home tutoring. But in the past five years, the number, range and rigor of such alternatives have expanded dramatically.

New opportunities created by digital technology have driven much of this expansion. The diversification of school markets in some countries also has contributed, allowing a greater role for community and parent voice and the potential—not often realized—for new solutions. Finally, greater attention to the needs of marginalized and disenfranchised students has stimulated the creation of alternative school and non-school models.

For the first time in education, we no longer have only a few discrete sites of innovation (in the old language, "experimental schools") but the beginnings of a transformation movement.

Our challenge is that this movement appears to be progressing in the absence of universally recognized design principles for 3.0 learning. The current drivers are less than ideal, on most occasions creating only partial solutions or limited change. Moreover (perhaps as a consequence of the lack of recognized principles), there's little evidence of a systematic approach to the study, evaluation, synthesis or scaling of promising new practices—or of agreed upon criteria by which systems can make meaningful assessments about how "promise" should be judged.

For system leaders in GELP, who are in the vanguard of this nascent movement, there is an urgent need to develop such principles so that new learning opportunities are practical expressions of Education 3.0.

The GELP design principles seek to address this by bringing together research evidence and the best of emergent practice into a set of criteria that are both ambitious and practical. To illustrate how GELP arrived at these principles, let's explore three unstoppable forces driving Education 3.0 and some of the most promising current models and practices to emerge from them.

THE LIBERATING POTENTIAL OF TECHNOLOGY

The explosion of online learning is one unstoppable driver for change. While educational *content* has existed in digital form for decades, the increase in online courses, or even whole learning platforms, brings revolutionary potential to anywhere, anytime learning.

While MOOCs (Massive Open Online Courses) have garnered the most media attention, we're also witnessing more computer-mediated learning *within* schools. In a practice widely termed "blended learning," an ever-growing number of students now learn partly in real-life groups and partly through online work.[79] Though no one has been able to fully track numbers, blended learning is a discussion topic among educators around the globe. It is estimated that China has 600,000 students learning at least partly online, while the US has 70 to 80 so-called hybrid schools[80] that combine in-person and online instruction.

National and state initiatives to digitize aspects of public education could accelerate such efforts dramatically. South Korea has progressed furthest in this direction, with pilots of "SMART schools" underway that vastly increase the flexibility and efficiency of the learning process.[81] Brazil, Mexico, Russia and Turkey also have announced or begun large-scale projects to digitize textbooks; both Australia and New Zealand have national platforms to support the use of online content.

Given these conditions, it would be easy to view blended learning as a wave that is already cresting; we need only wait for it to break and hope that educators can ride it. But as it stands, relatively few schooling and learning models are using blended learning toward truly transformative ends. In the US (where entire virtual schools have existed in Florida since the 1990s), the first hybrid schools essentially bolted together the online courses of virtual schools with traditional classrooms, into what are aptly called "bricks and clicks" schools.[82]

Distance learning and virtual schools are unquestionably important innovations, making learning accessible to people in a wide variety of contexts. This is especially true in countries where the number of well-prepared teachers will never catch up with the number of young people. In India, for example, the Digital Study Hall puts distance learning to work in reverse: The "teachers" travel to different schools in the form of DVDs of model lessons, which facilitators in rural areas learn from and use with their own students. Intriguingly, in the very different environment of New York City, similar strategies offer more students access to less popular areas of study. Here we see distance learning solving previously intractable problems, and that is a desirable thing.

But distance learning was an invention of the last millennium—an adaptation of a process of learning that did not radically alter content or methods. Similarly, the main *blended* learning approaches tend to represent a solution to a particular problem within the existing model of schooling: such as resources for remediation or drop-outs. But these approaches do not affect the core model of schooling and therefore the *nature* of the learning experience. As with all ubiquitous expansions, much of it is poor quality even though the best is potentially transformative. Technology-enabled learning is only as good as the learning principles that underpin it.

However, amidst the plethora of schools and systems making shifts of one sort or another to digital learning, a small but growing number of sites are developing innovative ways to use connectivity in service of 3.0 learning.

At Discovery 1,[83] founded in 2001 in Christ Church, New Zealand, students get the foundational skills they need in "must-do" sessions of intensive literacy and numeracy preparation. But technology's primary role is to provide a structured environment for learners to take control: Digital technology is the toolkit that enables rigorous, student-led projects and a whole variety of other "can-do" activities.

At their best, technology-enabled schools power learner agency. This is the hope of South Korea's new Smart Schools, the first of which are currently being piloted. The philosophy behind equipping students with tablets and creating a more open learning platform is that it will allow learners to pursue individual interests at their own pace rather than being beholden to a "once and for all" examination.[84]

Digital and online technology makes possible greater individual choice but can also help learners better integrate school with their lives. Growing attention to learning outside school offers greater flexibility for students to link up with other resources and programs in their communities—an enabling feature for more authentic, more connected learning.[85]

At Virtual High School, Ontario[86] students decide when to study, when to be assessed, when to hand in assignments. The school's only role is to respond to student needs by empowering them to make their own choices. Teachers are accessible online, by phone or email, so students can study anywhere as they see fit. VHS has 5,000 students. The critical optimizer, of course, is the enabling power of technology, but this is a design centred on personalization and agency.

DEMAND-LED MODELS: OWNERSHIP OF LEARNING AND THE TRANSFER OF POWER TO LEARNERS

Virtual High School—despite its name—shares key principles with a much older form of alternative education: democratic schools.[87] Where best conceived, these models prioritize learner ownership. Democratic or alternative schools are growing in number and have achieved greater global spread: The Alternative Education Resources Organization has member schools in 42 countries.[88] South Korea, for example, despite a very high performing system, is seeing an increasing number of students choose alternative schools once limited to "drop outs." With 40 of these schools now in Seoul, the appetite for an alternative approach to learning is mirrored at the primary level, where Jeju's City Bomulseom School drew attention in 2011 for being a cooperative, student-led model.[89]

The need for new kinds of learning also is changing the model of some home-schoolers, who are forming groups and finding partners in local institutions.[90]

The PLACE (Parent-Led and Community Education) initiative in the UK is an example where home-schooling has connected with mainstream school, but where "school" is simply a service offer—one of many available resources in the local palate of learning opportunity. Half the home-schoolers in the locality (approximately 150) subscribe to PLACE. They have rooms above a shopping precinct in the town from where the program is coordinated and led. Learners are offered a range of learning experiences, where a week in an artist's studio or a month's study on a farm might be juxtaposed with school-led or school-based courses and opportunities. PLACE students are not constrained by forced attendance or by age. They progress and are assessed at their own developmental rate, often learning alongside siblings and/or adults, connecting with peers through technology and study support groups—resulting in a potent model of personalized, demand-led and integrated learning. The school link, though, is profoundly significant. Being "on-roll" at the school means that this previously unfunded home schooling cohort qualifies for government funding—which is then devolved to PLACE to fund the initiative.

Leading democratic schools illustrate how an environment that allows for personalized learning can be co-created with communities.

The Lumiar Institute in Sao Paulo, Brazil, demonstrates the value of connecting school and community in this way. At Lumiar parents and students play a key role in school decision making, and the weekly assembly, The Circle, serves both a deliberative and celebratory function for all partners. The school has no lessons, fixed timetables or traditional teachers. Half the staff work as "advisors," supporting students to select and design three or four projects that they would like to work on each term. The other half are "masters," who work part-time to bring particular skills or expertise that they introduce into the students' projects, so ensuring content rigor and relevance.

Drawing on the resources of a community in this way helps to connect the foundational stages of schooling to learners' later needs to support themselves. In the changing world of work, all individuals must be prepared to "learn a living." This phrase formed the title of a study carried out in 2012 by the Innovation Unit for the World Innovation Summit on Education, examining cases around the globe of innovation at the interface of learning and work.

The most successful new forms were built upon learner agency, developing not just foundational skills but also the skills to problem solve, form solutions and ultimately *be* part of the solution. The methods that developed these capacities were highly contextualized in a learner's immediate environment, drawing on and responding to the resources and needs of the community.

While there is a valid drive for universal standards and skills to prepare learners for a globalized world, this study reminds us to balance such standards with attention to how individuals can develop their own paths and solutions over the course of a learning life. Emphasis on the need for personal and co-created learning environments can help to achieve this balance.

WORKING WITH NON-USERS

Alternative provision—models that have evolved in response to current "non-users" of schools—provides a rich vein of innovation because these examples have often found ways to engage the disengaged. And the disengaged could be seen as the canaries in the coalmine, those for whom the current system stopped working— just as it is now not working for hundreds of thousands more: the actively and passively disengaged through to the rising number of unemployed graduates.

Certain of these models have found long-standing success and point to a number of principles for making learning relevant and engaging.

City As School, in Manhattan, led by Alan Cheng, is a so-called transfer-school—last chance schools for those rejecting, rejected by or falling behind in the formal system. Informed by evidence from research on student drop-outs in which 65% felt that they had no deep relationship with an adult, 80% felt that lessons were not engaging and 90% wanted more real world experiences, the City As School model was consciously designed to address each of these. Their answer to the question, "How do we prepare students for life after High School?" is "Make it more like life after High School." All students experience internships and intensives—extended community-based learning experiences— where the classroom is relocated to community contexts. The school year and week is flexibly structured, success is redefined and assessed differently and a partnership with Apple supports on-going innovation in both adult and student learning.

The chance to connect learning to the wider world, to personalize from passions and to make choices is crucial—just as it's crucial that they happen in combination. Structured opportunities to access a range of wider experiences helps students connect their learning to things that "matter," fostering engagement and aspirations. This is understood by the growing range of schools that connect students to real-world contexts—the workplace, community projects, campaigns or service—such as the public high schools of Nashville, Tennessee, which each now incorporate high quality vocational experience alongside a high school education.[91] This district-level initiative is just one of a host of new realizations of the long-standing US model of "Career Academies." [92]

"Connected Learning"—where students form relationships with individuals from real world institutions and settings—is now being championed at a transnational level by a network of educators, researchers and professionals developing methods and programs for linking learners to experts worldwide.[93] The need to prepare active citizens by combining learner-driven experience with real world challenges and collaboration is mirrored in the most forward thinking vocational programs in the world—programs such as SENAI in Brazil, Sweden's Hyper Island (now operating in five countries[94]) or Denmark's Kaos Pilots.[95] As with the cases featured in *Learning a Living*, these equip people of all ages not to take a job, but to take on the future.

In a world that now requires everyone to be an adaptive learner, the boundaries between traditional, alternative, remedial and vocational education are blurring. Instead, new models embrace a set of common aspirations: providing learners with rigorous support for skill and capacity development, either in a classroom or online, combined with real world experience and passion-driven projects and authentic assessments that can demonstrate their learning.

THE ROLE OF LEARNING RELATIONSHIPS

But there's another ingredient. In a recent exercise[96] to find ten "schools for the future," the most outstanding examples nurtured deep relationships with the learner. Whether through advisory structures, having teachers see fewer students for longer time periods or using external mentors and other figures, these schools inspire, guide, support and challenge young people. The Lumiar Institute of Brazil; Big Picture Learning; High Tech High in San Diego; the Kunskapsskolan schools;

Human Scale Education[97] in the UK and the Small School movement across the United States all build, albeit in different ways, around the centrality of learning relationships.

Even India's Digital Study Hall, cited earlier, has at its heart not the technical solution of shipping DVDs around the country but the creation of an informed foundation for in-classroom mediators, who provide the motivation, guidance and mentoring that learners need to be engaged and to develop.[98]

Both research and practice underscore the importance of deep relational support—each student being profoundly known, both as a person and as a learner—as a feature of an emancipatory yet rigorous approach to learning for individuals from all backgrounds. Yet it is notably absent in many existing secondary education approaches. Summarizing the importance of such relationships in a single principle, however, is unnecessary—all the other principles uncovered below require placing a greater priority on deeper, more diverse or more wide ranging relationships.

DESIGNING A WAY FORWARD

So we know learning requires deep learner engagement. We have insight into what types of engagement promote powerful learning. And we have seen that there are around the world, in GELP jurisdictions and beyond, some models and approaches that hold promise.

For all that, most school systems around the world have not been designed to optimize learner engagement. Instead, all kinds of barriers stand in the way, resulting too often in models that are:
• **Divided**: teachers and content divided by subjects, students by notions of future prospects;
• **Standardized**: students educated in batches by age, following the same standard curriculum, all assessed at the same time;
• **Isolated**: schools designed to keep students inside, and the rest of the world out, with struggles to involve families and a reluctance to partner with other schools;
• **Hierarchical**: students seen as recipients of learning, with teachers the dominant resource; and
• **Technology islands**: technology deployed mostly to support existing practices for efficiency gains, and students tending to outpace schools in the adoption and consumption of technology.

In contrast, the six design principles that follow can and should be used by policy-makers and system reformers to create and explore new designs for 3.0 learning environments.

Informed by extensive practical work and horizon-scanning carried out by the GELP team and drawing upon the work of GELP system leaders in their jurisdictions, as well as extensive research, the six principles for designing Education 3.0 indicate *we need educational and learning environments that are:*

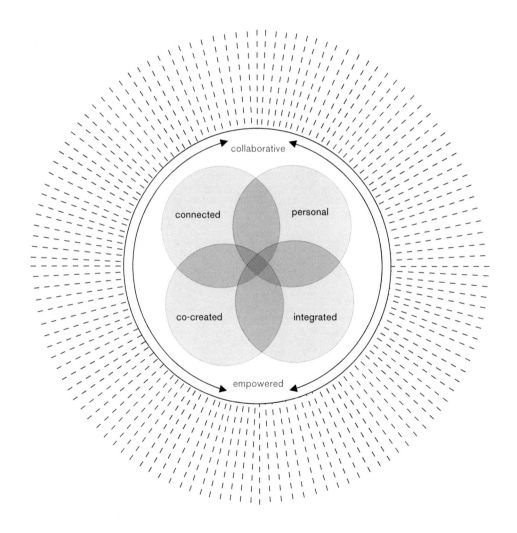

Personal: build from student passions and capabilities; help students to personalize their learning and assessment in ways that foster engagement and talents;
Integrated: emphasize integration of subjects, integration of students and integration of learning contexts;
Connected: connect with and use real-world contexts and contemporary issues; are permeable to the rich resources available in the community and the wider world;
Co-created: recognize both adults and students as a powerful resource for the co-creation of community, the design of learning and the success of all students;
Collaborative: build into the working norms opportunities for adults to work collaboratively and contribute to a professional knowledge base; and
Empowered: use the potential of technologies to liberate learning from past conventions and to connect learners in new and powerful ways—with sources of knowledge, with innovative applications and with one another

The first four principles are *driving* principles that inform new designs. The last two are pervasive, *enabling* principles, without which ambitious new learning designs will not work. These capacities have been shown to undergird more engaging learning environments. Collaborative adult learning and enabling use of technology are hardly surprising—yet they function sub-optimally in most current designs. We place the six together as design principles to recognize a continuum of "ends" and "means" that lie at the heart of good design.

These principles are interdependent; you can't pick and mix. That being said, interpretation of these principles likely will lead to plurality, not conformity. There is no one new model that derives directly from the principles; there will be many.

In fact, the cases above illustrate just that point. Around the world there exist multiple new schooling and learning models consistent with these principles. They range from new schools to home education partnerships, virtual schools and small schools.

PUTTING IT ALL TOGETHER: ENGAGEMENT AND INTEGRATION
This chapter began by emphasizing the importance in the 21st century of learner agency and engagement. It moved on to illustrate examples that show promise in this regard. Drawing from evidence, experience and research, GELP has proposed six design principles for 21st century learning systems. These six design principles

must be applied as an interdependent whole to enable Education 3.0. Now, let's look at an existing model that illustrates this interdependence.

In San Diego the High Tech High schools have for a dozen years now been guiding close to 100% of their open-access intake to college through a model based on great projects, strong relationships and the three integrations: of head and hand; school and real world learning; the "rigor" of the academic and the "applied" of the vocational.[99] High Tech High is not driven by technology— although the ambition of the work is ubiquitously enabled by technology. A hidden driving feature instead is the embedded nature of adult learning—one hour a day of shared collaborative planning and study time alongside high visibility teaching through which the problems of practice are resolved and made public professional knowledge.[100] Additionally, a core emphasis for the High Tech High family of schools is deep learning relationships with the learner. This is a means by which they support students to succeed, to personalize and increasingly pursue authentic work independently and interdependently and to create beautiful exhibitions. The pedagogical model is driven by authentic (real world) interdisciplinary projects, which play to the passions of teachers and students and allow for elements of co-creation and for students to personalize their work. The collaborative learning norms that characterize adult learning at High Tech High are replicated in the peer-to-peer support norms and learning protocols embedded into the study of projects.

EVOLUTION AND REVOLUTION COMBINED

For most jurisdictions, the task ahead is neither evolution nor revolution, but both. Leaders must address the "split screen" challenge of improving the existing system while promoting a radical redesign of learning. They must simultaneously design as if there were no existing schools *and* rapidly develop the existing school system to be fit for the 21st century.

The GELP design principles can help guide this dual journey. They represent a set of aspirations and goals for powerful learning. But they also highlight a series of levers—practical features that schools and organizations can adapt—to provide gateways to deep-seated change in the ethos and practices of learning environments. So:

• **Personalize**: focus on passions, learner ownership and engagement;
• **Integrate**: prioritize integrated, real-world-related projects;
• **Connect**: use the community by creating permeability both ways;
• **Collaborate**: build in time for adults to co-design learning and teaching;
• **Co-create**: emancipate the latent potential of learners as co-designers and peer-to-peer supports; and
• **Empower**: allow technologies to liberate ambition and support collaboration.

Most of the examples in this chapter are adaptations that push out or away from conventional "school" practices. Only a few, more radical examples—for example the PLACE initiative—start from a completely different place and rethink what "school" could be. All gain strength and coherence through their integration, by reforming old and building new relationships. The power of these levers offers both clarity of purpose and an architecture for scaling and diffusing practice—a discipline for the adoption and adaptation of promising new models of learning.

NOTES AND SOURCES

[69] Gibson, W. (4 December 2003). The Economist.

[70] Benjamin, H. (1939). The Saber-tooth Curriculum. (McGraw-Hill, New York).

[71] Eisner, E. (2004). "Preparing for Today and Tomorrow", in Educational Leadership, Vol. 61, No. 4, pp. 6-10. See also (April, 2002) The Kind of Schools We Need, Phi Delta Kappan, pp . 576-583.

[72] See: http://purposed.org.uk/, http://www.guardian.co.uk/teacher-network/2012/feb/09/purpose-of-education-debate and http://www.tes.co.uk/article.aspx?storycode=6075468

[73] This quote is attributed to the anthropologist (and aphorist) Margaret Mead in a 1980s work on education. Although she would have spoken them some decades ago, it was at the beginning of a period of change in how knowledge is created during which they would only become more relevant.

[74] Hattie, J. (2008). Visible Learning: A Synthesis of Over 800 Meta-Analyses Relating to Achievement. (Routledge).

[75] Cross, K. P. (2005). What Do We Know About Students' Learning and How Do We Know It? Research and Occasional Paper Series, University of California, Berkeley.

[76] Adapted from the Paul Hamlyn sponsored Learning Futures program: http://www.innovationunit.org/our-projects/projects/learning-futures-increasing-meaningful-student-engagement

[77] Among many educational innovation and futures orientated strands of work, the OECD Centre for Educational Research and Innovation (CERI) published in 2010 The Nature of Learning: Using Research to Inspire Practice, designed to inform education policy and practice, based on evidence, about the nature of future learning environments.

[78] For examples showing the continuing power of this approach, both in and outside traditional school models, see Ron Berger's work, An Ethic of Excellence: Building a Culture of Craftsmanship with Students (2003) and http://elschools.org/

[79] The Innosight Institute—probably the leading organization in studying and advocating for Blended

learning—defines it as: "any time a student learns at least in part at a supervised brick-and-mortar location away from home and at least in part through online delivery with some element of student control over time, place, path, and/or pace." (2011). The Rise of K-12 Blended Learning.

[80] Keeping Pace with K-12 Online Learning: An Annual Review of Policy and Practice tracks numbers of online learners in the United States; in 2012 they included 'Blended learning' in the title of their annual report, but stated that it was impossible to collect accurate numbers. http://kpk12.com/reports/ In the only nation or state to have gathered comprehensive numbers, a survey in California estimates that 45% of districts or charter schools offer online courses. http://www.centerdigitaled.com/classtech/Blended-Online-Learning-California.html

[81] http://english.keris.or.kr/es_ak/es_ak_100.jsp

[82] Silicon Valley Education Foundation. http://toped.svefoundation.org/2010/05/11/bricks-and-clicks-a-new-hybrid-school/

[83] http://www.discovery1.school.nz/

[84] http://english.keris.or.kr/es_nw/es_nw_100.jsp

[85] Sefton-Green, J. (2013). Learning at Not-School. (MIT Press). http://dmlhub.net/sites/default/files/Learning%20at%20Not-School.pdf

[86] https://www.virtualhighschool.com/ A TEDx talk by Stephen Baker, Principal of VHS, can be seen at: http://www.youtube.com/watch?v=EPzskdaQ8K4.

[87] A wide variety of schools fall under this label, but a key feature most share is that they try to give greater autonomy to the student. This usually arises from being a "democratic school," where the community and parents share in decision-making and endorse a student-led model; or from being an alternative provision for students who have "dropped out" of traditional schools and whose starting point demands re-engagement and different choices.

[88] http://www.educationrevolution.org/blog/list-of-aero-member-schools-organizations/

[89] http://www.jejuweekly.com/news/articleView.html?idxno=2210.

[90] See for example http://www.nytimes.com/2012/03/15/arts/artsspecial/museums-welcome-home-schooled-students.html?_r=0. The Riverside School in Gujarat, India, founded by mother Kiran Bir Sethi in 2001, is also a highly successful example of a parent bringing together outside elements to create an alternative school. http://www.schoolriverside.com/

[91] http://www.mnps.org/Page68146.aspx

[92] http://www.aypf.org/documents/092409CareerAcademiesPolicyPaper.pdf

[93] http://clrn.dmlhub.net/

[94] http://www.hyperisland.com/about

[95] http://www.kaospilot.dk/

[96] Hampson, M., Shanks, L., and Patton, A. (2011). 10 Schools for the 21st Century and 10 Ideas for 21st Century Schools. Innovation Unit. www.innovationunit.org/resources/10-schools-21st-century

[97] http://www.hse.org.uk/

[98] http://dsh.cs.washington.edu/info/descr_pedagogy.html

[99] http://www.edutopia.org/high-tech-high-larry-rosenstock-video

[100] http://www.hightechhigh.org/projects/ and

http://www.hightechhigh.org/unboxed/issue9/editors_welcome.php

BEYOND THE FRAGMENTS: SCALING AND DIFFUSION

As we have seen, one-off examples of radical new practices are not hard to find. We can point to outlier "model schools" that incorporate key aspects of Education 3.0 or break through traditional models to better serve their students. Scattered around the world are powerful instances of learning on the very edge of or entirely outside formal education systems.

Pay a visit to any jurisdiction in GELP—or indeed any city, state or country in the world—and system leaders and school principals can show you groups of students with personalized learning plans, instances of project-based learning, demonstrations of performance-based assessments, pilot sites of technology-enabled learning. Hundreds of educational websites with thousands of learning resources cater to all ages and subjects. Young people everywhere can find learning experiences that are more interactive, more engaging and just plain more fun.

Yet these exemplars remain stubbornly isolated and fragmented. Fully integrated and consciously designed examples are few and far between. Most formal learning for young people, the bulk of most education systems, remains largely unaffected. What will it take to move from pockets of exciting new models to transformed systems; from extraordinary opportunities, educational outcomes and life chances for the lucky few to a connected system that delivers for the many?

There is no inevitability here: Innovations within the formal education system spread or diffuse painfully slowly. System leaders in GELP know that how they act in the present will determine the nature of their resulting, future systems.

If they can encourage and support teachers and principals to be open to new models of learning and to collaborate with students, parents and external partners in developing these models, and *if* they can implement effective mechanisms for diffusion so that the models are widely available, *then* the system can be transformed from within. Failure to act on any of these dimensions could result in large-scale providers outside of or on the edge of the current system simply overtaking system transformation efforts.

But this is difficult and complex work. Moving from isolated examples of great practice to widespread great learning has evaded educational systems for decades, including some of the highly successful systems in GELP. The reasons for this can be understood by exploring some of the mistaken assumptions or "myths" that underpin current approaches. Collectively, these illuminate the principles behind the need for change in how system leaders approach diffusion. A fundamental shift in teaching and learning requires a parallel shift in the processes of scaling and diffusion. We need to move beyond traditional command-and-control strategies for compelling change, to ones that focus on vision, engagement, co-design, collective work and building communities of practice.

MYTHS OF DIFFUSION
An extensive body of research exists on sectors and organizations with high rates of diffusion. From this we can distil five "myths" that pervade thinking about diffusion in education.

Myth 1: Diffusion is (just) an informational problem
Most approaches to diffusion in education assume that evidence and providing good information will convince or persuade practitioners to adopt a particular innovation: hence the reliance on ever-glossier pamphlets, ever-flashier websites, ever-larger exhibitions and conferences and beacons, training workshops and demonstration sites to present and "disseminate" innovations. While these may attract significant audiences and readerships, follow-up studies tend to show low rates of uptake.

In their frustration with the limited effectiveness of these mechanisms, politicians and system leaders often turn to "command and control," instructing schools to adopt particular new practices. This can work where the innovation is a specific product or package; for example, phonics for literacy. But if the innovation is more radical, requiring behavioral or organizational change, such as developing teachers as facilitators of learning rather than purveyors of knowledge, then "command and control" is more likely to result in surface compliance (re-badging old practices in the new language) than in deep commitment.

As Emily Klein and Megan Riordan observe in the adjacent field of professional development, "for most teachers the decision not to implement professional development revealed some conflict from participants—although they generally believed in and theoretically understood why a practice was promoted, they rationalised that their context was unique and not conducive to applying the strategy."[101]

In addition, teachers often reject new approaches, even when proven, as the risks of implementation are perceived as too great in what are often high accountability, tightly regulated environments.

Myth 2: The dominant mechanism of diffusion is transfer
Educators mistakenly assume that innovation spreads by transfer from the school where the innovation developed to other schools. By comparison, studies of other sectors show that one of the most powerful ways in which innovation, particularly radical innovation, spreads is not through transfer but by the innovating organization scaling up, providing services or products to a larger proportion of the population, and displacing the organizations that have not adopted or developed the innovation. Motor cars did not replace horse-drawn transport by cart manufacturers becoming car manufacturers!

Myth 3: Innovation and diffusion are separate and sequential processes
Educators often talk about developing or piloting a new practice and then, if successful, rolling it out across the system. Sectors with more rapid rates of diffusion tend to talk more of prototypes than pilots. Whereas pilots are generally seen as test-runs of completed innovations and involve a limited number of people and locations, prototypes are intentionally unfinished designs that embrace a wide

range of potential adopters and users in refining and enriching the development and testing out its applicability in a variety of settings. The earlier in the innovation process potential adopters and users actively engage with the prototype, the more likely diffusion will accelerate. Diffusion and diffusion strategy are not something to be done *after* an innovation has been developed but need to be thought about from the very beginning.

Myth 4: Increasing the pipeline of innovation will increase diffusion

Government policies and strategies for innovation in education, where present, tend to focus on the supply-side, which is concerned with stimulating the generation and development of innovative practices. Many countries and states now have prizes and awards for "innovative teaching" or new educational games or the "educational innovator of the year." While this has helped increase the flow of innovation, policymakers have paid insufficient attention to the demand-side of the equation: rewards and recognition for those teachers, departments or schools that adopt or adapt innovations rather than originate them themselves.

Myth 5: Professionals are the (only) key agents of diffusion

Most efforts to encourage the diffusion of innovation in education focus on teachers. It's true that teachers more likely trust their professional colleagues than others, be they government officials, academics or vendors. However, in sectors where innovations spread more rapidly, it is often user demand that drives diffusion. Even in medicine, where greater claims are made that evidence drives changes in practice, a major factor in the speed at which new drugs come into widespread use is the strength of the relevant patient networks and organizations.

From Myths to Realities

So what does all this mean in practice for the scaling and diffusion of innovations in education? For moving from pockets of innovation to transformed systems? For ensuring that *all* young people have the learning opportunities to survive and thrive in the 21st century? Given that the traditional means and mechanism of diffusion have proven to be of limited effectiveness, what approaches are emerging that have greater potential?

Based on the research on diffusion and on what works in other sectors, system leaders in GELP are developing and implementing strategies that comprise one or more of the following components:

• a powerful and compelling case for change;
• nested communities of practice, engagement and interest;
• networks and chains;
• enabling policies and system dynamics;
• mobilizing demand; and
• building social movements.

A POWERFUL AND COMPELLING CASE FOR CHANGE

The first chapter of this book outlined why transformational change in education is essential. In every jurisdiction, system leaders intent on transformation have developed a powerful and compelling case for change as a critical first step that helps to create and maintain receptivity to developing and adopting new and more effective models and practices. Such cases necessarily depend on the context and circumstances of a particular country or city. For example, in the Finland and South Korea teams (countries that consistently lead in current international comparisons), GELP members stress how the skills required for jobs in the coming decades will differ from those in the previous century. New York City's case focuses on inequalities between different social groups and how end of school test attainment is not the same as college and career readiness. Brazil focuses on extending educational opportunities to the entire population, while Australia references the pervasiveness of media and technologies in young people's lives. Several jurisdictions make reference to findings from neuroscience about how children and adults learn.

Despite this range, the best and most compelling cases for change have common features. They:
• combine a rational and emotional appeal; personal stories as well as surveys and statistics; and learning from experience as well as from research;
• address global factors but translate these to local conditions;
• critique the current system as being appropriate to the past but inadequate for the future;
• present a truly inspirational vision of what transformed education and learning could be like;
• appeal to a range of audiences or stakeholders: educators and education leaders, students, parents and communities, politicians and policy-makers; and
• use a variety of formats, with short and arresting videos perhaps the most

common for general usage.[102]

As transformation proceeds, as new models and practices become established, these cases for change are augmented with evidence of the actual outcomes achieved. Model schools, such as those being developed in Chaoyang (Beijing Academy) or Rio de Janeiro (GENTE), provide further inspiration. The compelling case becomes more and more the compelling proposition, but never leaving behind the reasons why change is needed.[103]

NESTED COMMUNITIES OF PRACTICE, ENGAGEMENT AND INTEREST

As the compelling case for change becomes more widely promulgated, more and more educators and entrepreneurs are called to action.

But radical innovation, the development of new models and practices, is hard and complex work, despite moments of elation and enjoyment. And while it is *possible* within individual schools and settings, transformation is more likely to occur, more likely to be effective and more likely to be scalable, when it is done collaboratively, in "communities of practice" that bring together potential innovators in a structured, supported and facilitated environment where they can:
• share research and knowledge;
• work together to use disciplined innovation methods;
• draw on the expertise of relevant partners; and
• learn from each other about overcoming obstacles and barriers.

Such communities of practice, frequently with different names, have emerged in many jurisdictions. They are perhaps most clearly articulated and structured in New York City's iZone360[104] or in the UK's Learning Futures[105] program funded by the Paul Hamlyn Foundation.

As we have seen, diffusion happens faster if potential early adopters[106] are engaged in the development and innovation process itself rather than being seen as recipients of "finished" or proven innovations. In several educational jurisdictions and other sectors, these "communities of engagement"—also known as "collaboratives"[107] and "networked learning communities"[108] —have been used to great effect.

Potential adopters are critical friends to the developers, enriching the innovative practices and simultaneously working through how the emerging practices would work in their context. This overcomes the "not invented here" syndrome and helps to make models and practices more transferable and scalable. Engaging a wider constituency like this also broadens the base of innovation capacity and capability, scaling the ability to innovate as well as scaling particular innovations and integrating them into new whole school models.

While these nested communities of practice and engagement are powerful means of accelerating the early stages of diffusion, in order to stimulate further reach, they need to be surrounded by "communities of interest." These communities are populated by individuals and organizations that are interested by the case for change and want to be kept informed of developments. In this space, newsletters, websites, conferences and workshops are all useful. As models and practices get more developed, tried and tested, and codified into protocols and standard operating procedures by the communities of practice and engagement, the community of interest are ready recipients. This is especially likely if the innovators have been authorized or legitimated to act on behalf of the system as a whole, as well as by their school or locality.[109]

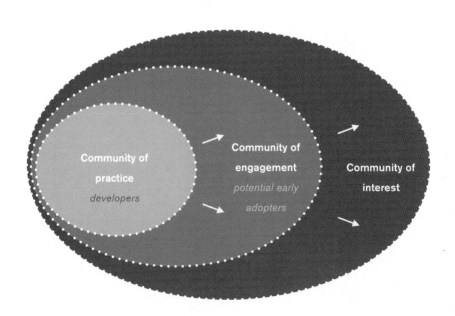

In many ways, the Global Education Leaders' Program (GELP) itself exemplifies many of these features. GELP started with teams of system leaders from four jurisdictions working together—with support from partners—and using frameworks and relevant methods, the case for change and the vision for 21st century learning and education in their context and circumstances. Subsequently, GELP has steadily recruited teams from other jurisdictions, and the scope of work has shifted to issues of planning and implementation of the actual transformation, with increasing collaboration through comparison, argument and interaction.

Nearly all the GELP teams have also created around themselves extended teams or groups of colleagues and collaborators back home.

Meanwhile GELP, as a program, continues to share its passions, purposes and activities through its website, conference presentations and publications—not least this book—to recruit new jurisdictions, organizations and individuals: to continue to build a global community.

NETWORKS AND CHAINS

The "nested communities" approach to diffusion emphasizes organic growth: Communities of practice synergistically develop new models, attract and enfold early adopters and draw in an ever wider circle of interest and influence. There is no one model of 21st century learning. Over time these communities may well split, like the division of cells, into separate nested communities, each clustered around one particular model.

Over the last few years we have started to see the formation in many countries of new networks or chains of schools—some based on new models of learning (for example, Kunskapsskolan in Sweden, High Tech High in California, Big Picture in the United States, Canada, Australia, Israel and the Netherlands) and many based on refinements of more traditional models of education. These chains can exist wholly within public systems, be independent but operate within public systems or live in the private sector. Some are based on strict adherence to a set of protocols and high fidelity to a particular model. Others offer considerable flexibility according to local circumstances but are shaped by a set of guiding principles or values. Taken together these networks and chains create the diversity for real parent and student choice within an education system.

All these networks and chains are also mechanisms for taking good and emerging practices and specific models to scale through:
• collaborative practice development;
• sharing of technological platforms, resources and leadership expertise; and
• enhancing the learning choices available to students and the career and development opportunities available to staff.

Recent evidence[110] suggests that networks and chains tend to have better results when they have a common governance structure, i.e. when they are relatively "hard," are based around profound and well-founded assumptions about learning and enable periodic physical, face-to-face coming together of staff and of students as well as frequent virtual connection and collaboration. In other words, networks work best when they are social as well as technological networks.

This network and chain phenomenon is a sign of education systems gradually taking on some of the common features of sectors that have high rates of diffusion of radical innovation. These include the non-profit sector in the US or the healthcare sector in Germany and the media, fashion, software and pharmaceuticals sectors globally.

It is instructive to see what other characteristics such sectors have for clues to what would further enhance scaling and diffusion in education. Also apparent are:

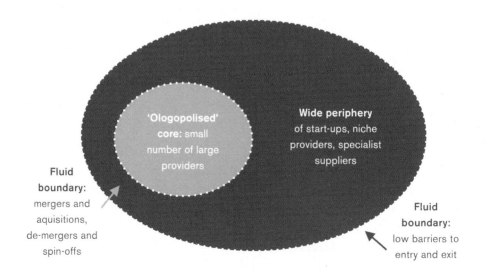

• an "oligopolised" core: a small number of relatively large players competing for shares of the market—arguably, in education these are the embryonic networks and chains seeking to attract students;
• a wide heterogeneous periphery of niche suppliers, specialist providers and start-ups—with regard to the latter, it is interesting to note that many jurisdictions, both within GELP and beyond, have opened up their systems to new entrants, for example 'free schools in the UK' or 'charter schools' in the US; and
• fluidity across the boundaries:
  - between the core and the periphery: mergers and acquisitions to increase the size of the core and core players; spin-off and de-merger activity to create new models and greater specialization; and
  - on the edge of the system: relatively low barriers to entry, enabling new entrants and start-ups, and relatively low barriers to exit, enabling the displacement of under-performers, outdated models and failed start-ups.

There are two more features to note. Other sectors nurture much of the radical innovation and generation of new models in the periphery, or in spin-offs from core players when ideas are too radical for the host organization. But it is the core players—in education's case, the networks and chains—who, through merger, acquisition or absorption, can and do take these innovations to scale —though often core players cling onto outdated models and are gradually displaced by successful and expanding new entrants.

This takes us back to one of the tensions highlighted at the beginning of this chapter, which permeates much of the debate and policy on the transformation of education.

In many countries, large commercial players who were not in the education market at all or were suppliers of educational resources are developing or using technologies to become education providers in their own right, sometimes in collaboration with individual schools or networks of schools, sometimes with the assistance of national or state governments and sometimes marketing directly to students. These players already operate at scale; they are at-scale organizations. For them, as potentially for any start-up or new entrant, technology is a vector of scaling and diffusion. As we saw in *Toward a Learning Ecosystem*, corporations and for profits like this will continue to develop and so cannot be ignored.[111]

SO WHAT CAN SYSTEM LEADERS DO?

It is highly plausible that one of the impediments to scaling in education, one of the factors in the low rate of diffusion within education systems, has been over-regulation and the lack of attention to sector dynamics.

ENABLING POLICIES AND SYSTEM DYNAMICS

The fundamental question for politicians and government officials is whether current policies and policy frameworks enable or hinder, support or impede the creation and scaling of models and forms of learning that will equip *all* students with the skills, knowledge and dispositions to survive and thrive in the 21st century. Are the funding and accountability regimes, the policies for teacher recruitment and development and the curriculum and assessment frameworks conducive to or barriers to transformation?

Some of these issues can be addressed through critical self and peer review by policymakers.[112] However, several jurisdictions—for example British Columbia—are beginning to use the experience of the educational innovators themselves to reveal the conditions that promote or impede the development of 21st century learning. They're also harnessing the expertise of teachers and students in developing policies and frameworks. This "bottom-up" policymaking fits well culturally with notions of students taking greater ownership of their learning. Just as 21st century teachers facilitate rather than direct learning, so 21st century government officials facilitate rather than direct policymaking.

Mobilizing Demand

Much of the above discussion about stimulating diffusion has focused on the providers of education. Yet, as we discussed in Myth 5, in organizations and sectors with high rates of diffusion, the involvement of "users" and "user" networks is critical. Students, their parents, carers and communities, employers and post-secondary education are, or at least should be, the beneficiaries of 21st century learning. Engaging with them to mobilize demand for such learning can be a powerful way of surmounting barriers, countering opposition and overcoming institutional inertia.

This is most effective when these stakeholders, their networks and organizations engage not just as "consumers" (though student and parental choice can be a potent driver of change) but as active agents in building the case for change, in articulating the vision, in designing and developing learning experiences at the level of new models and practices and in the actual day-to-day learning of young people.

Building Social Movement
All the above methods for stimulating diffusion, taken together, present a very different approach to system-wide change and scale from conventional means of transformation.

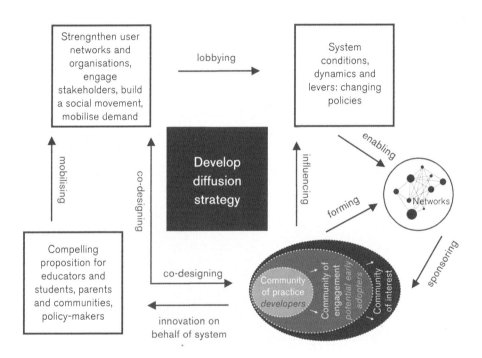

Rather than the trench warfare often associated with system reform, this approach relies more on organic growth, akin to the building of a social movement:[113] a movement that bonds together educators and students; teachers and academics; schools and communities; practitioners and policymakers; principals and system leaders; educational and social entrepreneurs; and public, private and non-profit sectors in the common endeavour of creating learning, learning opportunities and learning organizations that equip *all* young people with the knowledge, skills and dispositions to survive and thrive in the 21st century.

As with other social movements and campaign efforts, this provides mutual

support to those struggling with the inevitable barriers and resistances. It enables people to affiliate with each other in a common cause and to engage at different levels, from receiving a newsletter to actively developing practices and policies, to responding to "calls to action" and compelling narratives. Social media and communication and collaborative technologies can accelerate and amplify such movements.

Such movements are beginning to emerge in several countries and provinces, in Brazil, Australia and British Columbia among others, uniting teachers, students and parents, schools, post-secondary education, employers and foundations.

German ornithologists and animal behaviorists use the word *zugunruhe* to describe the restlessness to move of flocks of birds and herds of animals before migration.[114] Throughout the world, individuals and organizations are displaying this *zugunruhe* with regard to educational transformation. A social movement can harness this restlessness, give form to the transformation and sustain and accelerate the journey to truly 21st century learning and learning societies. It can, in the words of change theorist Gareth Morgan, "ride the waves of change," or as the planning academic Peter Hall says, "Go with the flow and bend the trends."[115]

Traditional means of "dissemination" will not enable the spread and growth of 21st century learning; at least not rapidly enough for young people to meet the challenges and issues of the coming decades. Educators must embrace new strategies and mechanisms tried and tested in other situations and sectors.
The next chapter turns to other elements of the transformational journey to which system leaders must attend for their travels to be effective: other elements needed on the road to transformation.

NOTES AND SOURCES

[101] Klein, E., and Riordan, M. (2009). "Putting Professional Development into Practice: A Framework for How Teachers in Expeditionary Learning Schools Implement Professional Development". Teacher Education Quarterly, Vol. 36, No. 4.

[102] For example http://gelponline.org/gelp-community/jurisdictions/australia or http://colegacy.org/elo/

[103] It is perhaps instructive to note that when a team within Amazon sets to work on a new product or service, the first task they are charged with is writing the media release for the launch.

[104] http://schools.nyc.gov/community/innovation/izone/Innovations/izone360

[105] http://www.innovationunit.org/our-projects/projects/learning-futures-increasing-meaningful-student-engagement

[106] This term was first given currency in Everett Rogers' classic 1962 work Diffusion of Innovations. See Rogers, E. (2010). Diffusion of Innovations. (Simon and Schuster). p. 22.

[107] On collaboratives, see the work of the U.S.-based Institute for Healthcare Improvement, for example 'Collaboratives and Spreading Improvement: An Annotated Bibliography. http://www.ihi.org/knowledge/Pages/Publications/CollaborativesandSpreadingImprovementBibliography.aspx

[108] For a review of the international evidence for Networked Learning Communities, see http://networkedlearning.ncsl.org.uk/collections/network-research-series/reports/the-impact-of-networking-and-collaboration/nlg-a-review-of-international-accounts.pdf

[109] It is worth noting that there are some tensions between this nested communities approach to diffusion and the increasing desire in some jurisdictions for a randomized controlled trial (RCT) model of evaluation. RCTs require double-blind control groups with fixed boundaries; effective diffusion needs openness, blurred boundaries and different "dosages." The former can work, in certain circumstances (see Cartwright, N. and Hardie, J. (2012), Evidence-Based Policy: A Practical guide to Doing it Better, for "pilots"); the latter requires iterative "prototyping."

[110] Hill, R., Dunford, J., Parish, N., Rea, S. and Sandals, L. (2012). The growth of academy chains: implications for leaders and leadership. National College for School Leadership.

[111] It is in higher and post-secondary education where the tensions have become most apparent with private sector players and "MOOCs" (massive open online courses), from leading global institutions forcing an increasing number of universities and colleges to realize that they will need to transform themselves to survive.

[112] A GELP cross-jurisdictional working group, led by colleagues in Colorado, is currently exploring these issues.

[113] The work of Marshall Ganz is particularly instructive here. See, for example, his Leading Change: Leadership, Organization, and Social Movements in Nohria, N. & Khurana, R. (2010). Handbook of Leadership Theory and Practice (Harvard Business School Press). pp 527-568.

[114] We are grateful to Rod Allen, Assistant Deputy Minister in British Columbia, for drawing this to our attention.

[115] Morgan, G. (1988) Riding the Waves of Change (Jossey-Bass). http://www.eurometrex.org/Docs/Meetings/Barcelona_2004/Presentations/Sir_Peter_Hall.pdf

PATHWAYS TO POSSIBILITIES

System leaders in education must knit together and connect new models and practices emerging locally at a small-scale with wholesale system-level change. This is both an education issue—realizing the principles, processes, practices and new organizational designs of 21st century learning—and a transformation challenge of huge proportions. And it's a journey that few are navigating successfully.

School systems designed for a previous age have proved remarkably resilient and resistant to change—much more so than other organizational forms. There are no fully realized precedents in education: Put simply, while transformation is required, there's no consensus on how to do it.

We can, however, draw on insights from other sectors and from innovators trying out approaches at large and small scale. There are some common, and illuminating, lessons.

GELP's work with jurisdictions has produced a clear set of essential elements for successful system change that together form a "roadmap" strategy. Developed with and used successfully by GELP teams, the GELP roadmap tool and the process of using it has united jurisdictions around a clarity of purpose and connected them to a wider knowledge-base and frame of reference.

There is no single correct pathway (though there are many ineffective ones). The challenge for each jurisdiction is to develop a roadmap and strategy that results in a globally robust education system, meeting the needs of its young people now and in the future, that is nonetheless appropriate to its culture, circumstances, capacity and readiness for change.

COMPLEXITIES AND CHALLENGES OF SYSTEM TRANSFORMATION

Like most issues in this book, education system transformation is very much a work in progress. While a vast body of tools and techniques, knowledge and understanding in school improvement and effectiveness, and incremental innovation has been accumulated over the last fifty years,[116] most of it focuses on what might technically be called endogenous (within-system) change. There is not yet an equivalent body of evidence and practice with regard to exogenous change—the transformation of a system by the incorporation of outside factors or influences external to the system.

Instead, committed teams and individuals within and across jurisdictions are figuring this out as they go, informed by a sector knowledge-base that is weak in terms of holistic planning and prior examples of success. GELP's role has been to provide these leaders with access to good tools and knowledge about transformation, especially the experience of transformation in other sectors.

It is messy and complex, difficult and challenging work. It is complicated by the relationship of education to national and local politics, and often paralyzed by the challenge of re-aligning the expectations of disparate interests, such as parents, employers and universities. The South Korean education system, for example, is to a large extent driven by the entrance requirements and selection processes of its elite universities. To fundamentally change the system will involve not just changes within the universities, but re-setting the expectations of students, parents, teachers and policy-makers, and mobilizing the voice of Korean employers around their need for a differently skilled workforce.

Responses to such challenges are not linear processes that can be planned and implemented in the conventional ways of the past. They are iterative processes necessitating the capacity to learn, adapt and refine; to reinvent policies and strategies in the light of emerging practices and to re-work the relationships between different levels of the system—school and district, district and state/

province and organizations within and outside the formal education system.

And the system leaders undertaking this work need to have the ambition of scale, which can vary from daunting to almost overwhelming:

Number of 0-14 year olds

India: 372,447,588

Brazil: 49,163,753

South Korea: 7,964,640

Australia: 4,297,838

New Zealand: 881,040

Finland: 861,920

In GELP, where system leaders are committed to *doing* this work, we realized we needed ways to describe and analyze the complexity and interrelatedness of system transformation. We needed a tool to help system leaders connect knowledge about how they might proceed with plans for their own unique route. Together we developed a framework for strategizing, planning and journeying on a roadmap for system transformation.

The roadmap framework needed to be recognizably "GELP": That is, it needed to model the Education 3.0 vision and hold system leaders to the values and principles that identify and unite GELP as a community of practice. It also needed to be flexible enough to accommodate an enormous range of contexts, priorities, resource availability and so on.

MAPPING AND NAVIGATING COMPLEXITY—THE ROADMAP FRAMEWORK

You do not want to miss important elements in this highly complex process.[117]

Professor Okhwa Lee, GELP South Korea

Drawing on the foundational documents of GELP[118] and members' experiences of pushing forward transformation in their own jurisdictions, as well as case studies and research on transformation in other sectors, we identified 16 elements that have shown themselves to be essential to success. The elements include three that are specific to education—around curriculum, assessment and pedagogy— three that concern disciplined innovation in the service of transformation and ten that are generic to system transformation efforts across sectors:

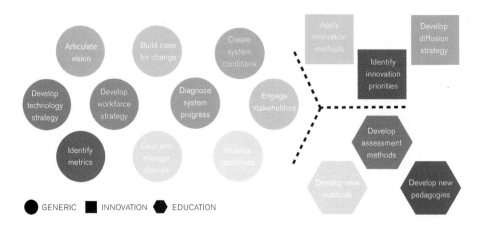

For each element, there are a number of sub-elements to consider:

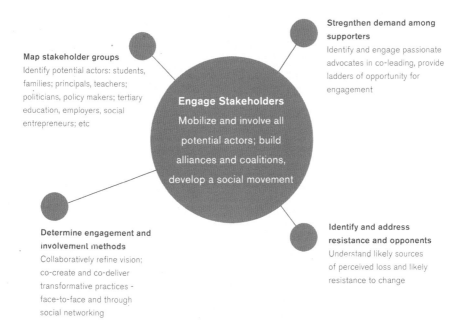

Map stakeholder groups
Identify potential actors: students, families; principals, teachers; politicians, policy makers; tertiary education, employers, social entrepreneurs; etc

Stregnthen demand among supporters
Identify and engage passionate advocates in co-leading, provide ladders of opportunity for engagement

Engage Stakeholders
Mobilize and involve all potential actors; build alliances and coalitions, develop a social movement

Determine engagement and involvement methods
Collaboratively refine vision; co-create and co-deliver transformative practices - face-to-face and through social networking

Identify and address resistance and opponents
Understand likely sources of perceived loss and likely resistance to change

Unlike many change frameworks used by major consultancies, the GELP roadmap does not attempt to define a set sequence. It is not a prescribed model or methodology. Rather, the roadmap provokes jurisdiction teams to debate and articulate the dependencies and relationships between the elements, informed by their understanding of their own context. It brings to the table best "public knowledge" about transformation from the theory, research and practice in other sectors that inform the choice of elements with the "practice knowledge" of local system leaders—their own leadership understandings and their unique knowledge of their jurisdictional context, which inform their individual roadmap.

COMMONALITIES, DIFFERENCES AND ISSUES

The GELP roadmap elements provide a common conceptual architecture, a set of lenses, through which jurisdictions' transformation journeys can be analyzed. A comparison of the journeys surfaces some insightful differences and common issues in the process of transformation; in other words, initial learning for other jurisdictions seeking to embark on this work.

Starting points – build the case for change and articulate a vision

Unsurprisingly, all jurisdictions start their journeys where this book began, with building and communicating a powerful case for change to develop an awareness and understanding among professionals and the public of the need, pressures and urgency for change. As described in the previous chapter, this is a necessary preliminary to efforts for diffusion and scaling. And nearly all the cases for change— from an initial plan created in 2011 by the state of Victoria to the Colorado Legacy Foundation's recent video campaign for Expanded Learning Opportunities[119] – incorporate many of the same sub-elements: international comparisons of performance, existing educational inequalities, student disengagement and dissatisfaction, the economic and social demands for new skills and behaviors, insights from the learning sciences (neurosciences and behavioral economics) and the possibilities opened up by new technologies and social media (which are themselves constitutive of young people's lives today and, arguably, shaping new patterns of human learning).

Though these various sub-elements are held in common, each jurisdiction gives greater or lesser emphasis to particular ones—for example, New Zealand stresses inequalities of educational outcomes between different ethnic groups, while Colorado emphasizes insights from the neurosciences—and interprets global trends in terms of their jurisdiction's particular context and circumstances. As well as this global and local feel, comparison shows that the cases for change are more powerful and reach more people when they combine the "rational" and the "emotional," using the stories and voices of students and teachers, parents and employers, to complement statistics and surveys.

Alongside, or shortly after building the case for change, system leaders have articulated a guiding vision of what 21st century learning might be like. This process, too, tends to be carried out in different ways according to each jurisdiction's context. In British Columbia, for example, an effort to source views from all of education's stakeholders within the public at large had begun prior to their engagement with GELP, leading to the development of the BC Education Plan.[120] In most jurisdictions, the vision is not a blueprint or a detailed plan but a provisional framework to guide development and innovation, recognizing that it will continue to be refined and modified as new practices and policies are trialed and tested.

In a sense, the case for change and the vision provide the framework and support for the journey as a whole and at each step: the case for change motivating and encouraging transformational efforts and identifying the problems and challenges to be addressed; the vision providing inspiration, setting a direction and establishing a beacon for when the journey gets rocky. Without a powerful case for change creating a sense of urgency, transformation will always take second place to the daily pressures of current practice. Without a guiding vision, efforts will be haphazard and uncoordinated.

However, when teams have met to discuss these elements and their sub-elements, they realize these are not events or episodes that kick-start the transformation process but themes that must weave their way throughout the journey, often re-articulated both to re-energize the work and to induct and enlist new entrants and participants.

Top-down and bottom-up—developing curriculum, pedagogy and assessment
System transformation cannot be mandated by government. Nor can it be built solely from the ground up. As well as building and communicating the case for change and articulating a guiding vision of 21st century learning, government has a key role as platform or broker; as stimulator, incentivizer and enabler. Government can target resources, set a facilitative policy climate and use accountability and reporting modifications to encourage new practices. But somehow government attempts to enforce transformation almost inevitably lead to surface compliance rather than deep commitment and profound change. Equally, while new pedagogies, curricula and assessment practices can be developed locally, they will not be sustained, embedded and spread without appropriate policy frameworks and infrastructure.

The close interdependencies between these three elements of curriculum, pedagogy and assessment make this an area where large-scale planning must attend to what might or might not be happening elsewhere in the system. For example,[121] in the roadmap section below, created by a jurisdiction reflecting on their current plans, the emphasis on fostering the development of new pedagogies as a driver for more personalized curricula and assessment holds obvious promise, but the omission of an embedded and equally pervasive workforce development strategy highlights a potential flaw.

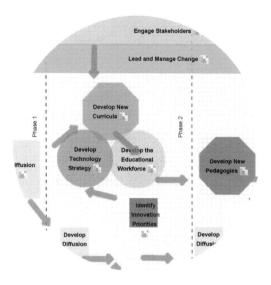

The balance of top-down and bottom-up approaches at any point in time critically depends on local circumstances. Australia and New Zealand—both well-developed and high-performing systems—have focused on centralized curriculum re-design, with varying levels of engagement with teachers, while encouraging the local development of new pedagogical practices.

The South Korea Government (which has presided over a remarkable improvement in performance in the last decade) in collaboration with the Korea Education and Research Information Service (KERIS) and the Education Broadcasting System, has chosen schools to pilot the first aspects of its SMART education initiative,[122] and KERIS is taking the lead to create model "future schools."[123]

The Central Board of Secondary Education in India, which has 13,711 affiliated schools, is revising its assessment frameworks to stimulate improving the quality of teaching and moving toward 21st century learning.

And the city of Rio and a number of states in Brazil, with a rapidly growing economy and a relatively under-developed school system, are investing heavily in developing and implementing Educopedia,[124] a web-based learning portal to bring high quality learning resources and the possibility of personalized learning to masses of students who currently experience highly variable teaching quality.

New York City has adopted a different emphasis. In the first phase of its transformation journey, after a decade of more conventional reforms that enabled it to be one of the world's fastest improving urban school districts, the Department of Education built a powerful and compelling case for moving from the "150 year-old industrialized classroom model" of teaching and learning to "mastery-based, student-centered learning" with four guiding principles: personalized learning plans; flexible and real world learning environments (multiple learning modalities, learning anytime, anywhere, on- and off-line, project-based); next generation curriculum and assessment; and new student and staff roles (advisor, tutor, mentor, designer, facilitator, peer-tutor, etc.).

But beyond the articulation of this vision, New York looked to aspirational schools in the city to develop the practices that would give life and meaning to the guiding principles.[125] It further supported this community of schools within the iZone, building a community of innovation and also incubating and accelerating their work on behalf of the wider system of schools.

Using the roadmap elements as an analytic framework for comparing different jurisdictions' approaches offers rich potential for learning. This is even more important as we consider parts of the transformation journey that present particularly complex challenges. The roadmap below, for example, was produced in a workshop where teams were asked to place red dots on elements that posed a particular challenge for them. In this case, two of the choices have proved prophetic for jurisdictions in general—applying innovation methods and developing a workforce strategy.

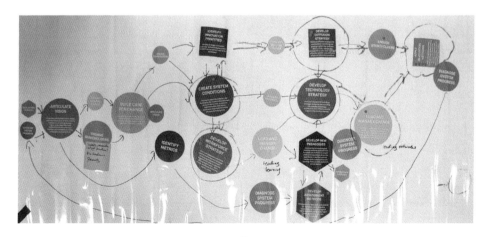

The next four elements we explore have all proven to present significant challenge. Even jurisdictions making extraordinary progress elsewhere are struggling to make headway partly because of the scale involved, but also because of the impact of change occurring outside the system. While their responses, current and future, will of course be different, all jurisdictions have something to learn from what is very much a work in progress.

Incubating effective new models and practice - Apply disciplined innovation methods

As we have seen, there is a veritable tidal wave of innovations in education. Thousands of schools around the world are developing new models of learning and different ways of organizing the school day and year, creating non-school based or school-as-base camp learning opportunities; global corporations and educational organizations are marketing new educational technologies and Massive Open Online Courses (MOOCS).

This tidal wave is indicative of a phenomenon common to all systems: As they approach a plateau of performance,[126] as external factors create the demand for different skills, products or services,[127] innovators both from within and outside the system are energized to innovate, to start to imagine and build components of a new system.

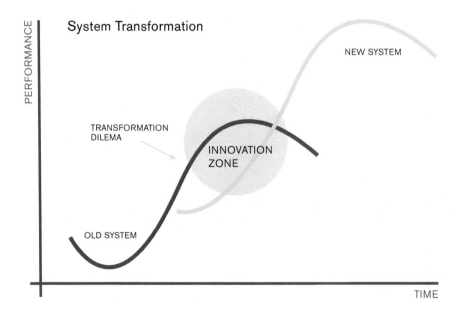

This energy is vital to system transformation, imagination, innovation and creativity. But for these innovations to be robust and effective, to mitigate and manage the inherent risks, translate ideas into reality, deliver real value and significantly better outcomes and have the potential for widespread adoption, *disciplined* innovation methods must be applied. A number of sectors have developed and refined such methods over the years, and although there is a plethora of frameworks and approaches, they contain many common features.[128]

For stimulating innovations:
• structured and systemic horizon scanning;
• creativity techniques;
• ethnographic research with "users"; and
• provocateurs from different disciplines.

For incubating innovations:
• service design;
• rapid prototyping;
• change management and capacity building approaches; and
• real-time evaluation based on theories of action.

Work with GELP jurisdictions has found that the use of one or more of these methods is apparent in most schools, districts and systems engaged in transforming learning. But they are most powerful when deployed together and set within a community of practice or an innovation zone, such as that in New York City, which brings together innovators from within and outside the education sector into a space where they can collaboratively develop new practices.[129]

Promoting innovation methods at the system level must be viewed in relation to the other innovation elements of the roadmap: identifying the priorities for innovation and developing a diffusion strategy. As explored in the previous chapter, creating 21st century education through innovation requires developing individual solutions and scaling them, creating a culture, and instigating system dynamics and policies that foster and support innovation across a system. This process is intimately connected to workforce development and leading change elements, and building a social movement that advocates for and supports the development of 21st century learning. Here, again, the importance of seeing the system interdependencies of the 16 elements of the roadmap as part of a holistic

strategy is key and can augment the impact of initiatives to improve technology, curriculum, pedagogy and openness.

Big opportunity, big challenge—Developing a technology strategy

This brings us to a unique potential accelerator of transformation. Earlier chapters have explored some of the ways in which ubiquitous digital technology can be a profound enabler and driver of 21st century learning.

Just as plumbing and wiring are essential and taken for granted in a modern house, so availability of digital resources, easy access to a readily navigable world of content knowledge and powerful mechanisms for collaboration are vital underpinnings of learning in the 21st century. But, just as no-one—except perhaps for plumbers and electricians—would describe a house in terms of its circuitry and pipework, so Education 3.0 cannot be described purely in terms of the technology.

This has posed a set of considerations and perhaps even dilemmas for system leaders in GELP—most important, it highlights the need for a technology *strategy*. On the one hand, there is an argument that system leaders can never stay ahead of technology developments and that, regardless, technology will be adopted when and where it should be. Yet while there will always be some people, especially younger people, who will adapt their behaviors and ways of working to the possibilities offered by particular technologies, this poses two risks. One is the ever-growing divide between digital haves and have-nots; the other is the divide between young people's technology-enabled habits of learning outside school and what is allowed within it.

To facilitate the uptake of new opportunities across their systems, jurisdictions that were at the leading edge of transformation often developed—with technology partners—their own learning management and support systems, for example Ultranet in Victoria, Australia,[130] or Desire2Learn in New York City.[131] Recent years have witnessed many commercial offerings enter this space, and the choice for system leaders has increased. The effect of this has been to make strategic choices more difficult rather than less. It is an area where cross-jurisdictional intelligence and collaboration will be of service and, at the time of writing, a working group of GELP members who are particularly exercised by this challenge has been established.

An allied issue is that technology alone cannot drive the development of new practices. While there are examples where new technologies are enabling newly adapted behaviors and ways of working, in many cases the technology has simply been incorporated into existing routines.[132] Any informed 21st century technology strategy will focus, like the Barefoot College in India or the Centre for Digital Inclusion in Brazil,[133] on harnessing young people's capacity to learn, on their dexterity with new technologies, on fostering new levels of engagement and connectivity and on the liberating power of peer-to-peer software. Hard- and software acquisition will need to be in service of this.

Acquisition cannot be ignored, however. Technology strategy has become more complex as the nature, price and ownership of technologies have evolved. In the early days, computers in schools tended to be clustered in computer suites or labs. Gradually they became scattered across and embedded in classrooms. Now many, although definitely not all, students have powerful mobile devices enabling them to communicate, collaborate and access information, learning resources and relevant applications. Throughout the world, schools are still trying to figure out how best to incorporate this potential while preserving security, privacy and a focus on learning and ensuring that students without these devices have equitable access.[134]

These complex considerations, and the experience of the jurisdictions in GELP, have been captured in sub-elements within the GELP roadmap tool:

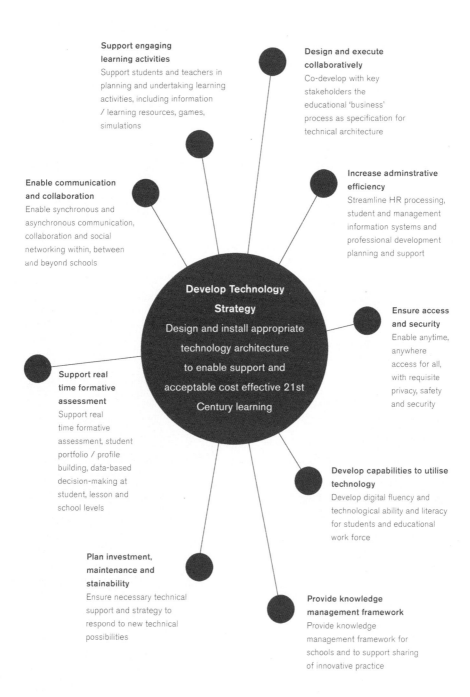

Support engaging learning activities
Support students and teachers in planning and undertaking learning activities, including information / learning resources, games, simulations

Design and execute collaboratively
Co-develop with key stakeholders the educational 'business' process as specification for technical architecture

Enable communication and collaboration
Enable synchronous and asynchronous communication, collaboration and social networking within, between and beyond schools

Increase adminstrative efficiency
Streamline HR processing, student and management information systems and professional development planning and support

Develop Technology Strategy
Design and install appropriate technology architecture to enable support and acceptable cost effective 21st Century learning

Ensure access and security
Enable anytime, anywhere access for all, with requisite privacy, safety and security

Support real time formative assessment
Support real time formative assessment, student portfolio / profile building, data-based decision-making at student, lesson and school levels

Develop capabilities to utilise technology
Develop digital fluency and technological ability and literacy for students and educational work force

Plan investment, maintenance and stainability
Ensure necessary technical support and strategy to respond to new technical possibilities

Provide knowledge management framework
Provide knowledge management framework for schools and to support sharing of innovative practice

As with all the elements, decisions about appropriateness and configuration of the sub-elements will depend on ambition and contextual considerations. Equally true, this element cannot be seen in isolation. A strategy for new technology is severely limited unless digital immigrants are prepared to engage with it.

The bedrock of transformation—Workforce development

All research on change management emphasizes that building the capacity of the workforce is critical.[135] No matter how compelling the case for change and how inspiring the vision, without developing the capacity of the workforce, anxiety, frustration and resistance will grow. There can be no change in how young people learn without significant change in what adults do.

In transformational change (and education is no exception), building capacity is not just an issue of skills development—whether in the use of new educational technologies, or working with students to develop their personal learning plans, or a move to facilitation skills—important though these are. The role of teachers, their identity as teachers, their relationships with students and learning, their working and learning habits, all have to change fundamentally. This is captured but not fully explicated as moving from "purveyors of knowledge" to "facilitators of learning," or as moving from "deliverers of subjects" to "designers of pedagogical experiences." Teaching as the transmission of knowledge from one generation to the next has been an honorable professional identity for thousands of years. But in the 21st century world of super-abundant information and rapid knowledge access, as has been discussed in previous chapters, a set of more differentiated roles is required.

Attempts to develop teachers in this role are making some headway in Brazil, where the Teacher's Development School is creating new modules focused on preparing teachers for a transformed system. In Rio de Janeiro, as in Australia and the state of Victoria, efforts to prepare teachers to work with the respective system-wide learning platforms, have seen a substantial change in the way teachers approach learning materials—a prior step to new pedagogical practices.

However, the complex interdependency of educational systems presents a potentially confounding feature. Teacher preparation programs (often the domain of universities) and continuing professional development (with its plethora of external providers) themselves need transforming.

In the most advanced models, teacher development is integrated into new designs such that the daily experience of adults mirrors the new learning values applied to students—supporting processes of culture building and cultural change, building and developing new identities, thus liberating teachers to be engaged learners within a new professional identity.[136] New culture and new identities only become firmly embedded through developing and practicing new ways of working, new behaviors and new routines.

It is proving critical for system leaders seeking to transform their systems to engage deeply with departments of education in universities and other training and development agencies and bodies. In some countries, cities and states, this is proceeding well. In others cases these organizations have proved to be seats of resistance rather than agents of change. And it is noteworthy that where this has happened, groups and chains of schools have broken away and sought to build their own professional preparation and development processes.[137]

SHARED LEADERSHIP OF A SHARED VISION

It's really important to bring everyone together in a shared agenda and a common understanding… [the roadmap] is a visualization of the messy work of achieving a 3.0 vision.[138]

Linda Pittenger, Council for Chief State School Officers, United States

Education systems—and the schools and institutions within them—have proven to be very resistant to change. While the mission of transformation unites countries and cultures, the journey to 21st century learning is strewn with obstacles, setbacks, dead ends and pitfalls. In contrast, the real periods of triumph, achievement and progress can seem less obvious.

As the experience of countries and cities engaged in transformation shows, there is a paradox to this work. For it to succeed, every school, community, state, country or system must build this change on its own terms. There is no fixed pathway. At the same time, without a shared and clear roadmap that incorporates all the essential elements of transformation, success is unlikely. System leaders must find ways to connect and align people behind the overall vision of Education 3.0 and pull the right levers and strategies to move the work forward. This requires focusing on leadership as a movement rather than on individual leaders in order to build the system's capacity to innovate.

NOTES AND SOURCES

[116] See, for example, the work of Michael Fullan and Andy Hargreaves, Richard Elmore and Seymour Sarason in the U.S., David Hargreaves and Michael Barber in the UK, Brian Cauldwell in Australia and Per Dalin in Scandinavia.

[117] http://gelponline.org/resources/film-gelp-roadmap-tool

[118] Cisco. (2008). Equipping Every Learner for the 21st Century. http://gelponline.org/resources/equipping-every-learner-21st-century ;

Cisco. (2010).The Learning Society. http://gelponline.org/resources/learning-society ;

Leadbeater, C., and Wong, A. (2010). Learning from the Extremes. Cisco. http://gelponline.org/resources/learning-extremes ;

Hannon, V., Patton, A., and Temperley, J. (2011). Developing an Innovation Ecosystem for Education. http://gelponline.org/resources/developing-innovation-ecosystem-education

[119] Towards Victoria as a Learning Community. (2011). http://www.education.vic.gov.au/about/department/pages/learningcomm.aspx; Expanded Learning Opportunities Initiative, Colorado Legacy Foundation http://colegacy.org/elo/

[120] http://www.bcedplan.ca/assets/pdf/what_youve_said.pdf

[121] All examples from actual roadmaps are used anonymously with the permission of the creators.

[122] http://www.dtbook.kr/renew/english/index.htm

[123] http://future.keris.or.kr/

[124] http://www.educopedia.com.br/

[125] http://schools.nyc.gov/community/innovation/izone/About_Us/default.htm; http://gelponline.org/sites/default/files/resource-files/case_study_nyc.pdf

[126] See Michael Fullan's discussion of the situation in Ontario, in Fullan, M. (2012). Stratosphere: Integrating Technology, Pedagogy and Change Knowledge. (Pearson)

[127] Detailed arguments that the time for this demand has come can be found in Zhao, Y. (2012). World Class Learners; and Barber, M., Donnelly, K. and Rizvi, S. (2012). Oceans of Innovation.

[128] Fuller lists and details of each of these practices can be found from many sources, including www.innovationunit.org and www.socialinnovationexchange.org

[129] The work of David Hargreaves on collaborative practice development is particularly instructive. See, for example, www.education.gov.uk/nationalcollege/docinfo?id=177472&filename=a-self-improving-school-system-towards-maturity.pdf

[130] www.education.vic.gov.au/about/programs/learningdev/pages/ultranet.aspx?Redirect=1

[131] http://desire2learn.com

[132] Hence the inconclusiveness of much of the research on the effects of technology in education: Technology is not an independent variable.

[133] For full discussions of these examples, see Chapter 2 and Leadbeater, C., and Wong, A., (2010). Learning from the Extremes. Cisco. http://gelponline.org/resources/learning-extremes

[134] OECD. (January 2013). Trends Shaping Education.

[135] For a particularly comprehensive exploration of parallel issues in another sector, see System Transformation in Healthcare: A Realist Review. http://www.milbank.org/uploads/documents/featured-articles/pdf/large-system-transformation-in-health-care-a-realist-review.pdf

[136] For example, the State of Sao Paulo in Brazil has instituted a 10-year, multi-billion dollar public-private sector partnership to simultaneously develop a new curriculum with digital content and an associated teacher preparation program, to develop the capabilities and capacities of teachers to be facilitators of learning.

[137] Examples include the Graduate school of Education at High Tech High, which has an accredited master's program as well as its own teacher preparation programs: http://gse.hightechhigh.org/, or the Harris Academies, which similarly combines teacher development work and accredited programs across its Academy chain: http://www.harristeachingschool.com/36/experts-in-teacher-training

[138] The GELP Roadmap Tool: http://gelponline.org/resources/film-gelp-roadmap-tool

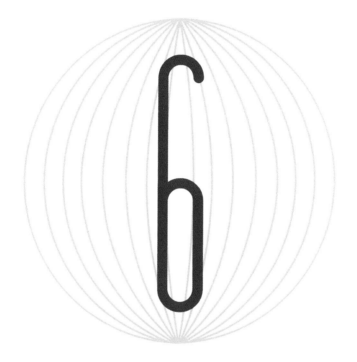

MOVERS AND SHAPERS: REFRAMING SYSTEM LEADERSHIP FOR THE 21ST CENTURY

Models of 20th century system leadership encouraged and prepared individuals to lead improvement in schools, systems and jurisdictions. Approaches and frameworks focused on the traits and behaviors of effective leaders. And leadership theories emphasized the role of individuals on system development.[139]

But the urgency and scale of the transformation facing today's leaders requires something more than incremental improvement; it requires them to lead radical and swift innovation in the service of whole-system transformation.

GELP is starting to reframe system leadership to reflect and take advantage of the learning possibilities enabled by new technologies, new models of learning, and a landscape filled with new providers. In GELP jurisdictions, system leaders must "be the change they want to see"; they must model the values and practices that are required to effect system transformation in their contexts.

These system leaders can emerge from anywhere—across sectors and age groups. As we saw in *Towards a Learning Ecosystem*, new entrants and providers are populating the educational landscape. As a result, some of the most exciting and successful leaders are not educators at all, but social entrepreneurs with a passion for learning and strong social values.[140] Most excitingly, many of the voices leading the movement to transform education come from learners themselves.[141]

DOMINANT LEADERSHIP THEORIES

Ideas about 21st century system leadership are new and at an early stage of development. But they attend carefully to the traditions that still dominate the theory and practice of educational leadership in most parts of the world: A ten-year project released in 1999 examined attitudes about leadership in twenty countries. It found a number of common traits regarding key leadership capabilities internationally. Charismatic/value-based leadership was strongly supported; team-oriented leadership was strongly correlated with charismatic/value-based leadership; and humane and participative leadership dimensions were almost universally endorsed.[142]

These characteristics are the foundation of outstanding leadership. System leaders with these qualities can be highly effective when leaders are motivating people toward a clear goal, proceeding on the basis of established knowledge and using effective structures to organize and manage their work. National and international policy discussions set the priorities for these system leaders: We want better teachers and teaching, higher standards for curriculum and assessment and tougher accountability provisions. Even now, limited attention is devoted to exploring alternatives beyond the traditional model of schooling and learning.[143]

20th Century System Leaders

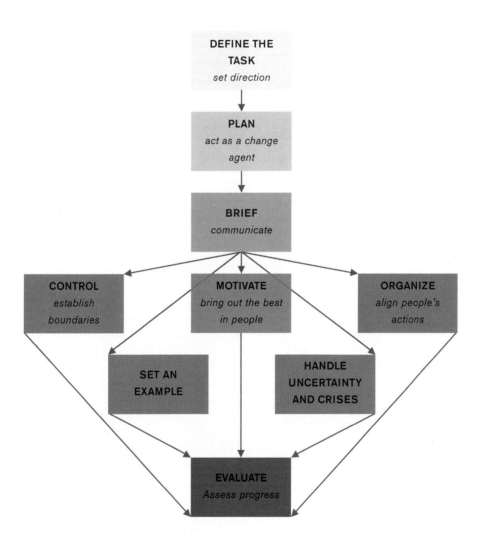

System leadership like this ably served the needs of the 20th century because it focused on the processes of improvement within a fixed and knowable paradigm. But the experience of GELP leaders is that the task-behavior frameworks, theories and models of the past century are inadequate for the challenges facing GELP jurisdictional teams today.

The leaders of 21st century systems, as this chapter suggests, must be "movers and shapers." They must employ a range of catalytic activities to engage fully with disruption and to move resources, people and ideas around proactively to shape the future of education, not just react to it when it gets here.

LEADING WITH A "SPLIT-SCREEN" ORIENTATION

In a period of transition, continuing improvement within the old paradigm will remain substantively and politically important. But leaders of education systems must also create the conditions for transformation, advocating for new policies and metrics that respond to the demands of the time. Their task is to manage a split-screen vision of system leadership—to both deliver on an improved present and to create the conditions for a transformed future of learning.

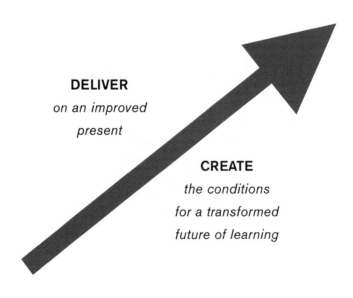

DELIVER
on an improved
present

CREATE
the conditions
for a transformed
future of learning

Examples from other sectors around the globe teach us that a focus on improvement alone rarely enables agile responses to fundamental changes in the environment that disrupt organizations and institutions.

Take for example the US postal service, where skyrocketing costs and a poor record of performance placed them at risk of extinction. Add to the mix a number of new entrants into the delivery space—United Parcel Service (UPS); Dalsey, Hillbloom and Lynn (DHL); and Federal Express—and suddenly the entire landscape of postal services changed. Or consider the seismic shifts in the phone industry over the last few decades: The rise and fall of Nokia, the extraordinary success of Apple and the alliances between huge multinationals such as Google and Samsung, who realised they'd need to combine technologies to survive. Now imagine you are leading the national provider of telecommunications in your country—AT&T in the US, for instance, or Telstra in Australia. With new entrants in the space and enhancements powered by technology, the landscape has changed dramatically, with multiple providers now offering differentiated services via more and faster technological innovations.

Those who genuinely want to improve education and learning opportunities have to reconsider what it means to lead in these demanding times. The assumptions of existing systems cannot deliver on the current goals of equity and excellence, let alone prepare learners for the future. As in many sectors, system leaders now have the task of equipping and supporting others to take up the challenges of "adaptive" work and change their orientation toward problems and solutions.[144] More specifically, to enable the new modes of learning that GELP jurisdictions seek at scale and to create the connections between opportunities in this new landscape, system leaders must move beyond an improvement orientation to create a pervasive culture of innovation within their system—and then connect this to other systems.

LEADING TRANSFORMATION

System transformation cannot be achieved by creating discrete innovations that are then "rolled out": It requires embedding the capacity for on-going innovation across a system. Moreover it requires the system itself to innovate. System leaders in GELP recognize that taking their systems into the future requires very different forms of leadership from them:

THAT WHOLE VIEW OF TRYING TO KEEP THE SYSTEM STABLE, BECAUSE SOMEHOW THAT'S A GOOD THING—I THINK WE BATTLE THAT, BUT THE KIDS WE'RE DEALING WITH DON'T HAVE THAT VIEW. [THEY'RE USED TO] CONSTANT CHANGE, WHICH STOPS IT FROM BEING CHANGE, IT'S JUST LIFE. [145]

Rod Allen, GELP British Columbia Team

Exactly what do system leaders do as they seek to create and sustain education and learning environments consistent with the demands of a complex and hyper-connected world? The first international studies of leaders of innovation in the public sector have begun to establish the qualities and behaviors associated with successfully sustaining innovations and an innovative environment.[146] Building on this research and work with system leaders in GELP, we have begun to identify the qualities and behaviors that form the foundations of effective 21st century system leadership for learning.

There are two cautions. First, individuals—however talented—cannot promote and sustain system transformation. In the 21st century, system leaders will succeed to the extent they engage others and grow and distribute leadership throughout their systems.

Second, the new qualities and behaviors described in this chapter do not mean the existing descriptors are unimportant. Leaders still will need these skills to improve their existing systems. The split screen metaphor emphasizes that for the transformational half of their role, system leaders in GELP need something different. This is why the concept of collaborative leadership teams is so important.

WHO ARE THE SYSTEM LEADERS IN GELP?

As a group, system leaders in GELP demonstrate a range of skills and qualities that recognizably characterize good—possibly even great—system leadership. System leaders in GELP are:

Systems-oriented: Active systems thinkers can see connections both within the organization they lead and across related organizations. They recognize that to advance transformation they have to strengthen the relationships between the sub-systems of their organizations. They acknowledge that they must orchestrate opportunities to connect other leaders and their organization as a whole to sources of learning. As system thinkers, they can conceptualize emerging trends, patterns, and issues across organizational boundaries that could facilitate or inhibit their strategies. These leaders actively work to translate their understanding in ways that help others with the ambiguity and uncertainty that comes with the innovation process.

For example, the GELP team from Australia supported the introduction of a new Australian Curriculum by brokering the contributions of policy makers, teachers and resource developers. Similarly in South Korea, the GELP team used the combined capacity of the organizations they lead to help develop a coordinated strategy for digitizing textbooks and curriculum materials across the entire country as a stimulus to the creation and adoption of new forms of learning and pedagogical practices.

Inclusive: Have an inclusive style that enables collaboration and provides the space for staff to take risks and build confidence simultaneously. They are team oriented in their approach and proactively build strong working relationships with key innovators across the organization. They structure, restructure and even dissolve teams as needed to create the appropriate architecture for innovation. Most importantly, they create an environment where "teaming" or "swarming"[147] as it appears in literature on 21st century skills can occur as needed and on a temporary basis around specific challenges.[148]

These leaders identify and release untapped energy within their organizations by engaging people from across organizational boundaries in the co-design process necessary for innovative problem-solving. A carefully designed work environment can help.

At the New York City Department of Education, central areas are equipped as spaces for temporary gatherings. An open floor plan allows for frequent interactions as staff at all levels move around during the day. In such an environment, system leaders are keenly aware that they must establish mechanisms and processes for dealing with conflicts and reconciling differences that will surface in a more horizontal organization.

In British Columbia, Canada, the Ministry for Education established a Department for Learning and reorganized both space and work arrangements for an entire floor of public servants to demonstrate that fifty years of existing practice had come to an end.[149]

Design thinkers: Know that innovation is powered by what people and organizations want and need in their lives. Often using direct observation, they develop deep understanding of the demand side of their work. They demonstrate empathy in their interactions by imagining the world from multiple perspectives. In this way, they connect problems and solutions in new and exciting ways. To do this, system leaders in GELP draw on design thinking; integrating different sources and types of knowledge, creating novel solutions to what appear to be intractable problems.[150] They are optimistic, recognizing that at least one potential solution is better than the existing alternatives and that progress is always an iterative process. They hold an experimental posture toward their work and are willing to pose questions and explore constraints in creative ways that can produce entirely new directions.

Entrepreneurial: Mobilize the human, social and financial resources needed for innovation. Working as social entrepreneurs both within and beyond their own organizations, successful system leaders in GELP are able to "grow the pie" by attracting talent to their organizations, crafting the trust conditions needed to promote innovation, and securing the financial resources to support the research and development aspects of innovation.

In Brazil and South Korea GELP teams have engaged with or even created companies to facilitate new projects that could not be pursued within their existing education systems. In working both within and beyond their own organizations, system leaders in GELP know how to appeal to the needs and interests of people, how to build a compelling case for change that signals the need for additional resources, and how to leverage under-utilized resources within and beyond their own organizations. They encourage an entrepreneurial attitude within their organization, creating the conditions to ensure iterative innovation can be sustained in the long term.

Strategic: Aware of how organizational policies and practices can either facilitate or inhibit transformation, system leaders are willing to confront and change government, system and organizational policies that stifle the creativity and energy associated with innovation. They identify government, system and organizational practices that impede an innovation culture. System leaders in GELP are able to establish the case for dismantling policies and practices that inhibit transformation and take responsibility for crafting policies and practices that facilitate it. GELP jurisdictional teams in Colorado and Kentucky have demonstrated their strategic orientations both by creating formal roles to lead innovation at the state level and by crafting new policies to stimulate innovation across their respective systems.

Grounded: Combine the confidence and humility central to successful, sustained leadership of all kinds. Grounded leaders understand who they are in their role— their strengths and weaknesses, their leadership style and their blind spots. They know that they have to project more confidence, and be more conscientious, than anyone else in their organization. They know that the best innovators are often people engaged at the practice level, and they figure out how to tap into the energy and creativity that exists across the organization.

System leaders in GELP are courageous and willing to confront unproductive conventions. They know that it can be lonely as a leader when you are promoting significant change for your organization. Innovation of any kind represents a shift in power and will draw opposition, so system leaders must maintain a tension between openness to advice and resilience.[151]

But over and above these qualities, the system leaders in GELP do — have to — take on a wider and more challenging role in their systems as they work together to shape the future of education in their jurisdictions.

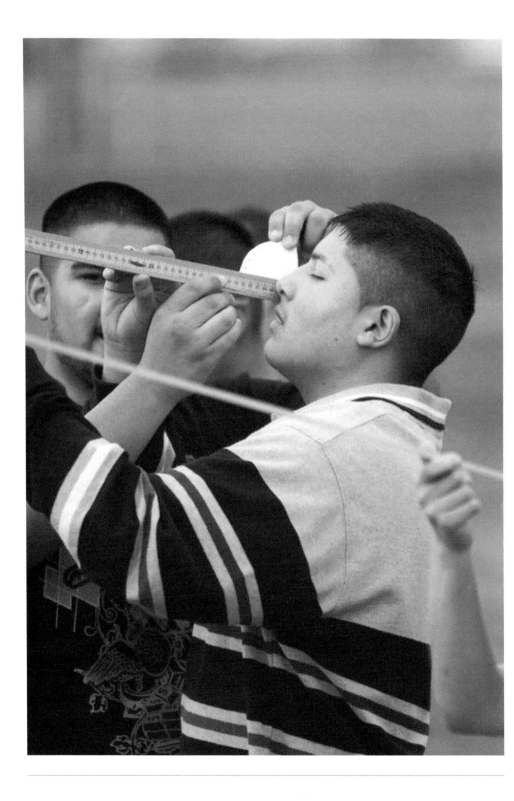

SIX DIMENSIONS OF 21ST CENTURY SYSTEM LEADERSHIP

Knowledge diffusion: 21st century system leaders are outward facing in their orientation, seeking to learn from others and promulgate the circulation of new ideas. They are intellectually curious about how things work, what motivates people and why certain ideas succeed and others fail. By asking penetrating questions reflecting a future view of the world, they use their inquiry skills to ferret out learning from their experiences. This outward-facing orientation takes them beyond their local environments into regional, national and international spheres.

In GELP we have been considering how individuals and teams of system leaders from extremely diverse contexts can work and learn together to mutual benefit. We've found tools and frameworks are powerful enablers that can support system leaders in translating their insights and learning into thought leadership in their own countries.[152]

"Social" networking: System leaders in the digital age build strong horizontal linkages across sectors and even across countries, which engage government leaders, social entrepreneurs, business executives, researchers and civil society leaders as partners in building innovations for education and learning.[153] Such linkages must be relational rather than transactional. They enable system leaders to build circles of support in pursuit of system transformation. These networks expand the resource base, as system leaders proactively seek out providers with particular expertise or different analytical models, or thought partners to help explore new ideas, develop new approaches and deepen understandings.

Working in teams across organizations allows leaders to experience the different domains of education—policy, pedagogy and politics—giving them better insight into how to play their particular role.

Susan Mann, GELP Australia Team

Cultural competence: 21st century system leaders move with ease beyond their comfort zones. They recognize the need to develop cross-cultural literacy to access the learning of others with different orientations from different systems. Engaging with the traditions, values and communication patterns of other professional and ethnic cultures is challenging. But it changes system leaders' world view; it sets them apart from those who are located firmly within a single cultural setting, gives them greater insight and credibility and models for others how work is organized and accomplished in a global environment.

IN OUR COMMUNITY, OUR VOICE AT THE TABLE IS SIGNIFICANT BECAUSE WE'RE APPROACHING THINGS WITH A GLOBAL VIEW, AND A FUTURE VIEW.

GELP British Columbia Team

Technology brokerage: 21st century system leaders are knowledgeable about the use of technology in learning and sophisticated in their use of technology in their own practice. To bring together technical and social innovators in productive and sustainable relationships, they need to understand the key aspects of new technologies and set themselves up with good sources of information about emerging technical innovations. Moreover, an ability to deploy social media helps system leaders to be vastly more effective in communicating their vision. In GELP, system leaders who strategically use Facebook and Twitter multiply their ability to communicate and therefore lead both within and beyond their organizations.

Political activism: 21st century system leaders are politically savvy. They understand both the micro and macro politics of working with people, working with organizations and working with systems. They leverage their knowledge about needs, interests and motivations to engage people in joining them in their transformation agenda. They use their knowledge about power and influence to build the alliances and coalitions they need both internally and externally to get things done. System leaders in GELP describe how the first-hand information they have from other jurisdictions helps them legitimize the political license they need to make changes in their own system. We have also seen successful use of provincial and national forums to create political buy-in for transformational efforts. System leaders recognize they are engaged in building and sustaining a social movement while they are working across the micro and macro elements of what it means to be "political."

Experimentalism:
At the cutting edge it isn't about emulation or catching up. Rather it's about having the confidence to experiment and then the capacity to make sense of the experiences.

Interview with system leader in GELP

In his recent evaluation of GELP,[154] Riel Miller offered the term "experimentalist" leadership to describe the system leadership he had encountered in GELP. These leaders can move beyond a general understanding of transformation. They engage seriously with a future vision of their education system not yet in existence to create the policy and design conditions that will give rise to the best versions of that future. The learning environment created by GELP helps system leaders to manage risk by experimenting outside of the existing paradigm, while making sense of what they learn from such experiments within the existing paradigm. Just as teams might visit one another's jurisdictions to learn from their contexts, system leaders in GELP construct a vision for the future, which they then "visit," to understand the implications of current decisions and actions for working toward that vision.

MODELLING THE CHANGE
Leadership for the 21st century enables others to take up the difficult challenges of adaptive and experimental work. This is necessary when leading in a time of transition: managing the movement from one set of practices to another and protecting the valued aspects of education while introducing new ones. It means attending to a range of tensions growing up within organizations and across systems. 21st century leaders clarify and balance these tensions but also harness that energy, while ensuring conflict does not prohibit action.

This is a new vision for 21st century system leadership and a challenging role for system leaders. But progress depends on the extent to which organizations, teams, communities of practice—not individuals—can adopt, embed and diffuse these qualities. System transformation simply cannot occur without the involvement and simultaneous transformation of every actor within the system. The ultimate system leadership task is to model the new habits, orientations and ways of thinking needed to enable more open, adaptive and innovative systems capable of transforming learning.

NOTES AND SOURCES

[139] Kellerman, B. (2012). The End of Leadership. (Harper Business).

[140] See Hannon, V., Gillinson, S., and Shanks, L. (2013). Learning a Living: Radical Innovation in Education for Work. (Bloomsbury) http://www.wise-qatar.org/2012-wise-book

[141] Examples of young people giving public voice to the need for a transformed education system include, in the United States, Goyal, N. (2012). One Size Does Not Fit All. (Bravura Books) and Listen, an upcoming film from 17-year-old Ankhur Singh: http://listenthefilm.wordpress.com/about/

[142] Project GLOBE. (1999). http://www.grovewell.com/pub-GLOBE-intro.html

[143] For example (April 2010). Innovation Based Systemic Reform (Education Evolving) http://www.turnexchange.net/greatlakes/archives/joe-graba---innovation-based-systemic.attachment/attachment/Joe%20Graba%20-

[144] Heifetz, R. A. (1998). Leadership Without Easy Answers. (Harvard University Press).

[145] Rod Allen, GELP British Columbia, quoted in Miller, R., (2013). Evaluating GELP: Towards Making Experimentalist Leadership Practical. Global Education Leaders' Program.

[146] Bason, C. (2010). Leading Public Sector Innovation: Co-creating for a Better Society Partnership; and Hay Group (2011). Leading Innovation in Public Services, Partnership for Public Services, D.C.;

Cels, S., de Jong, J. and Nauta, F. Agents of Change: Strategy and Tactics for Social Innovation. (Brookings);

Edmondsen, A. C. (2012). Teaming: How Organizations Learn, Innovate, and Compete in the Knowledge Economy. (Jossey-Bass); Spillane, J., (2006). Distributed Leadership. (Jossey-Bass).

[147] Austin, T., (March 2010). Watchlist: Continuing Changes to the Nature of Work, 2010 -2020. (Gartner).

[148] Edmondsen, A. C. (2012). Teaming: How Organizations Learn, Innovate, and Compete in the

Knowledge Economy. (Jossey-Bass).

[149] http://gelponline.org/resources/transforming-education-case-study-british-columbia

[150] Brown, T. (June 2008). 'Design Thinking.' Harvard Business Review.

[151] Moore, M. H. and Bennington, J. (2011). Public Value: Theory and Practice (Palgrave Macmillan); Cels, S., de Jong, J. and Nauta, F. Agents of Change: Strategy and Tactics for Social Innovation. (Brookings).

[152] Miller, R., (2013). Evaluating GELP: Towards Making Experimentalist Leadership Practical. Global Education Leaders' Program.

[153] Wilson, E. J. (2004). Leadership in the Digital Age, in Goethals, G. R. Sorensen G. J. & MacGregor Burns, J. (eds.) The Encyclopedia of Leadership, 4 vols.

[154] Miller, R., (2013). Evaluating GELP: Towards Making Experimentalist Leadership Practical. Global Education Leaders' Program.

SYSTEM TRANSFORMATION: A WORK IN PROGRESS

This book has focused largely on transforming the systems that provide formal learning for school age children, which is the responsibility of the system leaders in GELP.

But the transformation described in these pages encompasses government agencies, learning environments and organizations beyond schools that are poised to take a role in a more open learning ecosystem. In reaching out to these players, system leaders are starting to unlock opportunities for learning, assessment and credentialing that stretch beyond such conventions as age-based learning or fixed and inflexible places of education. In doing so, they seek to meet the needs of a more fluid landscape of learning for life and work. This is the learning society, and this final chapter will take up some outstanding questions fundamental to this shift.

Earlier chapters have suggested where the greatest opportunities and hindrances lie in transforming the education systems we have into the ones we want and need. A tool created by leading public management thinker Mark Moore might help.[155] Moore's theory of the strategic triangle holds that any creation of public value or innovation process—in this case, the wider and more relevant learning opportunities created by system transformation—relies on the interplay between the required *authorizing environment*, the *value proposition* of the change and the *operational capacity* to carry it through.

Considerable work from organizations around the world has gone into articulating the case for change in education and the new vision of better learning. There is therefore a strong public value proposition poised to break further into the public consciousness in many countries.[156]

This growing public demand is just beginning to affect the authorizing environment—the political leaders who set education priorities for nations, states and communities. Around the world political rhetoric is fixed firmly on improvements within the current paradigm, with national economic competitiveness equated with a narrow set of test scores. A major task for system leaders in GELP is to influence the political rhetoric—globally and locally—to create greater authorization for transformation.

Often in an innovation process the authorizing environment will have a tight relationship with the level of organizational capacity that can be applied to the work. However, this book demonstrates how strategic leaders and organizations have found capacity to put toward the process of transformation through a split-screen approach and partnering with the private and non-profit sectors.

For work toward Education 3.0 to continue, this additional capacity must grow. Creating Learning Societies is too big a task to be left to one portion of the public sector, particularly when many countries are grappling with economic austerity and

uncertainty. We have to allow a range of new players to join the wider ecosystem that creates learning opportunities. At the most radical edges of this expansion are communities, parents and learners themselves on the one hand, and for-profit businesses on the other. Increasingly these two constituencies interact in a marketplace in which formal public education is just one more commodity, one choice that consumers of learning can make.

Earlier chapters have addressed a number of the challenges and controversies that this analysis invites in setting out new roles for governments and system leaders. This chapter takes up the implications of these developments for education professionals and explores the nature of this market to set out an agenda for the next phase of thinking and action in GELP jurisdictions.

THE ROLE OF EDUCATION PROFESSIONALS

Teachers must be change agents in system transformation, particularly in the new ways they interact with learners. But to create the capacity for better and more interaction, accredited professionals in formal education settings may need to share learning facilitation with others. To make lifelong learning available to all, to reach out to those whom formal education struggles to serve, we need to embrace more varied forms of provision and create more roles for different actors.

This book has not addressed the process of transforming the education profession in detail, in part because the nature of the challenge is so dependent on jurisdictional context. GELP system leaders are considering the future of the profession in their jurisdictions and the potential for others to contribute to learning. But they are in the foothills of this process, and it is fraught with risk. Union unrest, political opposition and negative media campaigns are a reality in several jurisdictions. Most ministries and agencies are so tightly bound to the profession that it's proving difficult to unravel a thread, to identify a place to start.

System leaders in GELP have three key tasks in taking this work forward. They will need to:
• encourage teachers and unions to take the lead in spreading and expanding their knowledge as a profession and in changing the dynamic between learners, educators and the system—including acknowledging the shift toward fundamentally changed roles for teachers;

• support the development of professional expertise or expert bodies to develop pathways and opportunities for differentiated roles for educators; and

• foster the professional capacity to protect education's role as a builder of communities, values and culture, even as technology allows learners to direct their own activity.

IN THE MARKET FOR LEARNING

Innovations in tools, technologies and practices can fuel Education 3.0. These will emerge from a range of players: researchers, academics, non-profits and nongovernmental organizations, institutions of further and higher education, learners, communities and professionals—including teacher-researchers and edupreneurs. Increasingly the number and range of providers needed to sustain a learning society will arise from a demand-led market—a market that responds to parent or student choice.

Learning—like many other goods before it—has become commoditized. As a result, it is now provided by a vast range of actors, from Sony to the Khan Academy. Learning systems need to embrace this breadth—the contributions of companies and communities—and make it part of jurisdictions' efforts to create 21st century learning systems. This is not an argument for the privatization of learning systems. On the contrary, it is an argument for their expansion in provision, access and scope. Free entitlement to quality learning opportunities for all citizens is a key principle for GELP. But this does not mean the state as sole provider of learning or supply capture.

Yet there is a danger that pursuing quality through markets has a homogenizing effect that narrowly construes the criteria of quality. To counter this, successful education systems must respond to the needs of individuals and communities. In a context where providers range from large profit-making companies to smaller social enterprises, market pressures must not be allowed to overcome what is in the best interests of a community or a particular subset of learners. The core principle of personalization is not customizable methods by which learners achieve set outcomes, but the flexibility of learning goals themselves and the scope for learners to pursue their own ends.

Second, system leaders must protect and promote the best interests of learners and prevent a profit motive from reducing the quality of services. Leaders must construct system metrics and tools that help learners and communities navigate the market and exert real choice pressure that enhances quality.

Overall, the movement toward a more open learning ecosystem makes it all the more necessary that we measure what we value as opposed to valuing what we can measure. There is an urgent need to develop better metrics to track how systems are fulfilling such goals as equity, inclusiveness and learner ownership. But most centrally, the key objective, the very purpose of education systems in this century, needs to be redefined. Governments must negotiate the criteria for systems success within their own cultural context, in debate with their citizens. The difficulty of this process must not preclude it from receiving attention.

THE ROLE OF GOVERNMENT

This book argues that Education 3.0 requires a government role of standard setting and safeguarding, managing the changing relationships between learners, markets, providers and educators. More critically, however, moving from an education system to a learning society requires connecting and interacting with the other systems in play—placing education in the broader public service context of economy, society, equality and democracy. Only government has both the ability and legitimacy to retain, protect and enact this overarching vision.

Moreover, this is not a mantle that government can choose to pick up or not. The unstoppable forces for change are bringing a new landscape of learning whether we are ready or not, and governments can either respond passively and ineffectually to the threat of the new or take the lead to actively shape the future of the societies they serve.

Given that this work is complex and wide-ranging in scope, it is particularly affected by the nature of the authorizing environment in any particular jurisdiction. The pathway must be negotiated on a national level, but as first steps all governments and their education departments must attend to a similar set of questions:
• How can leaders—political and professional—move to a more authentic discussion of their societies' learning needs, rather than one which talks the talk of creativity, innovation and future but mandates mediocrity, conformity and control?
• By what processes can government both enable the diverse aspects of the

learning ecosystem to flourish and exert enough control to promote equitable access and protect the best interests of learners?

• Does government have a bigger role to play as stimulator or controller? Should its role in shaping Education 3.0 be restricted to reinventing professional preparation and development and changing the metrics by which success is measured?

• How can governments, particularly those with limited resources, exert influence over an increasingly diverse education without falling back on command and control measures that have traditionally stifled radical innovation?

Answers to these questions will differ depending on the jurisdiction and the level at which education is currently managed. Adopting the role of a platform may firstly require governments to rethink the balance between central and local control. As a general principle, the trend towards centralization for key indicators and infrastructure appears to facilitate greater ease of implementation of new technologies and the participation of market players. Other aspects, however, such as curriculum design and creating strategies for innovation, are likely to benefit from local control to be more responsive to the needs and aspirations of communities.

TRANSFORMING SYSTEMS - A MESSAGE FOR LEADERS ACROSS THE PUBLIC SECTOR?

A government prepared to take a role as enabler of Education 3.0 would be better equipped to meet the adaptive challenges of other sectors, too. In healthcare, social care, even penitentiary and public works systems, the pressures of demographic change and reduced public sector budgets, coupled with the opportunities of new technologies and new employment patterns, are producing similar calls for a change in the balance of responsibilities between governments, citizens and the private and non-profit sectors.

Therefore, just as we hope education system leaders in jurisdictions who are not members of GELP will learn from the experience of their work, we hope too that the lessons in this book are suggestive for leaders in other sectors, in the way we have learnt from system change efforts in health and social care.[157]

RUMORS OF MY DEATH ARE GREATLY EXAGGERATED

Mark Twain

This book ends where it started, with the words of a brilliant and disruptive thinker.

In all probability, in most parts of the world the "structures and strictures" of schools that Stephen Heppell points to in his "death of education" are likely to persist for a little longer. The corpse is not aware that it is dead.

So the question, in the near term, is what will the relationship of those institutions be to the wider learning ecosystem that is growing up around them? And how can we make certain that all that is good in formal education and the opportunity it represents is not lost in the rush to diversify or to disinvest?

GELP will continue to work as a diverse and growing community to find this balance and to manage the transition for the generation of learners now in school, at the same time as we plan and implement an exciting learning future for the next generation.

NOTES AND SOURCES

[155] Moore, M. H. (1995). Creating Public Value: Strategic Management in Government. (Harvard University).

[156] The past year has seen a notable rise in the number of books, documentaries and articles describing something akin to transformation of education. Many have already been featured in this book, but additional examples include Wagner, T. (2012). Creating Innovators: the Making of Young People Who Will Change the World; Is School Enough? (2012 documentary); Design For Change (2012) The I Can Book, Amar Chatra Katha publishing house, India.

[157] For an example of lessons from system level transformation in the health sector, see the aforementioned Best A, Greenhalgh T, Lewis S, Saul JE, Carroll S, Bitz J. (2012). Large-system Transformation in Health Care: A Realist review. InSource Research Group, British Columbia.

INDEX

31597886R00097

Made in the USA
Lexington, KY
17 April 2014